Paul Burns

REVISION PLUS

AQA

GCSE English Literature
Anthology Companion

Revision and Classroom Companion

Contents

How to Use the Anthologies

The Anthologies and the English Literature Course

If you are studying AQA GCSE English Literature, you may have been given copies of the two AQA anthologies: *Moon on the Tides* (poetry) and *Sunlight on the Grass* (prose).

Moon on the Tides contains sixty poems and *Sunlight on the Grass* contains seven short stories. You will not have studied all of these texts. The ones you have studied and need to revise depend on two things:

* which units of the course you are taking
* which texts your teachers have chosen to teach for those units.

Prose Anthology

Everybody takes Unit 1, Exploring Modern Prose. This is in two parts:

* **Section A: Modern Prose and Drama** – you can use the seven stories in the anthology, or a longer text – either prose or drama – selected from a list provided by the exam board.
* **Section B: Exploring Cultures** – you must use a selected set text, chosen from a list provided by the exam board.

Poetry Anthology

The poems are for use in Unit 2, Poetry Across Time, or Unit 5, Exploring Poetry. You will only take one of these units.

* For **Unit 2,** which is assessed by exam, you will have studied one of the four 'clusters' of poems (fifteen poems in all) in the anthology so that you can answer a question in Section A. You will probably also have looked at poems from other clusters to help prepare you for Section B, where you will be asked to write about a poem you have never seen before.
* If you are doing **Unit 5,** which is assessed by controlled assessment, your teacher has a wider choice of poetry. However, many of you will be using poetry from the anthology for this unit. The poems you have studied may be all from the same cluster or selected from different ones.

Poetry from the anthology can also be used for Unit 3 of the English Language course and Unit 3 of the English course.

Using the Anthologies

During the GCSE course, you will have been using your anthologies in class, underlining, highlighting and making notes. You will not be allowed to take your own copies into the exam or controlled assessment. Instead, you will be given 'clean' copies to work from. This will help you to focus on the question you are given, rather than trying to cram all your notes into the answer. Examiners have found that most students actually produce better answers if they are not bogged down by notes.

However, you do need your own copies of the anthologies for revision, so try not to leave them in school or lose them. The notes you have made in them are valuable because they are your notes, written in your own way and reflecting your own thoughts.

This revision guide is intended to complement, not replace, your notes. Some things you read here may be familiar. Other things might be new to you – or different from what you have been told. This does not mean that either your teacher or the author of this book has got it wrong. Different people can have different responses to the same text. This book is not designed to tell you everything there is to know about the texts, nor to tell you what you should think. Studying literature is all about developing your own response and your own point of view and, hopefully, this book will help you to do that.

Exploring Modern Prose

As part of your GCSE you will have to take Unit 1, Exploring Modern Texts. However, not everybody will have studied the same texts.

For Section A (Modern Prose or Drama), you may have studied a modern novel, a non-fiction text or a play. If so, you will not be answering questions on the seven short stories contained in the anthology *Sunlight on the Grass*.

If you have studied the short stories, you will need to revise all seven of them to give yourself the best chance of answering a question you feel comfortable with and can answer well.

When you write about your chosen text you will be expected to look at the following:

- **Ideas, themes and issues**: what the text makes you think about. The stories often have similar themes. For example, 'growing up' is a theme of both *The Darkness Out There* and *When the Wasps Drowned*.
- **Characters**: the people in the text; what they are like; how they act and react; and why. In some of the stories, for example, *My Polish Teacher's Tie*, the protagonist (main character) is the narrator. In others, we share the protagonists' thoughts and feelings even though they are not telling the story. Think about the other characters in the story – not just what they are like, but what they represent.
- **Settings**: where and when the action happens. Most of the stories take place in ordinary, familiar settings, but at times these places can be disturbing and unsettling. Others are set in less familiar places: Japan, Sudan and Malaysia.
- **Language and techniques**: how the writer gets all these things across to the reader using **form**, **structure** and **language**. For example, you might want to comment on: how the story is organised; whether it is written in the first or third person; the kind of language used; and the use of imagery and symbols.

In the following pages you will find information about the author of each story, a summary of each story and comments on the above aspects of each story.

In the exam, there will be a choice of two questions on the anthology short stories. Each question will be in two parts: the first about a named story and the second on a similar theme but about a story of your choice. You do not have to compare the two stories, so, in effect, you will be writing two short essays. You will have roughly twenty minutes in which to write each response.

Practice Questions

Answer one of the following questions in 45 minutes.

Question 1

Part (a) How do you respond to the character of Carla in *My Polish Teacher's Tie*?
Part (b) Go on to write about the way the main character is presented in one other story from the anthology.

Question 2

Part (a) How effective do you find the ending of *When the Wasps Drowned*?
Part (b) Go on to write about the ending of one other story from the anthology and how effective you find it.

Compass and Torch Elizabeth Baines

The Author

Elizabeth Baines was born in South Wales. She has written plays for the radio and stage as well as novels and short stories. This story was inspired by seeing a father and son walking on hills in Wales, but also draws on her own experiences and emotions.

Narrative

A young boy goes on a camping expedition with his father. His parents are separated and his mother's new boyfriend, Jim, now lives with her and the boy. The boy is very excited about the adventure and proud that he has remembered to bring a torch. His dad has also brought a torch. They stop on a moor, where there is a group of wild ponies. One of them approaches the car and the man tries to 'bat' it away. They get out of the car and the man gets the tent out of the car boot.

As they look up at the path that will take them to the brow of the hill, the man realises he has not brought a compass. The boy says that he too forgot his compass. They walk across the plain and set up camp on the other side under the highest peak. They eat and then, when it gets dark, go to bed. During the night the tent is surrounded by wild ponies. We are not told what happens next but for years to come the boy will be haunted by the experience.

Ideas, Themes and Issues

- **Growing up / Change**: the boy is only eight but this is a significant moment in his young life when things change (an epiphany). Life will never be the same again.
- **Family**: this is a traumatic time for the family. The parents separated a year earlier and the boy's relationships with his mother, his father and Jim are all difficult.
- **Father and son**: the most important relationship is that between the father and the son. The boy wants to be like his father and to be loved by him, but they are already losing touch emotionally.

- **Masculinity**: the father is trying to do what is sometimes called 'male bonding' – sharing an activity that he thinks boys would enjoy. The boy loves the idea of being a man like his father, but his mother mocks the plan.
- **Man and nature**: the wildness of the moors dominates the story. The ponies belong on the moors, but the boy and his father seem very weak and insignificant out in the darkness.

Setting

The story moves from the familiar setting of the boy's home to the moors where he goes camping with his father. The countryside is wild and empty and inhabited by wild ponies. The moors are notoriously dangerous for people who are unfamiliar with them and not properly equipped.

Although the story would seem to be set in the present, the last sentence indicates that in fact it is an incident recalled by the boy many years later when he is grown up.

Characters

The boy is never named. He is eight years old and we learn a little about his family, but he could be any boy in that situation. He admires his father a great deal and wants to impress him and to imitate him. He is very excited, but nervous, about the trip.

Dad might be seen as a typical father who no longer lives with his son. He is anxious to give the child a good time and has planned an adventure for him, but his ex-wife thinks he is reckless and is just showing off. In fact, the man has not prepared properly for the expedition and soon realises it. He tries to appear in control and cheerful for his son's sake, but he feels that he is becoming a stranger to him. We never learn what happened to split up the parents, but the man is obviously not happy: the story refers to him as being an expert at blocking out pain.

The **mother** might seem to have got over the split because she has a new boyfriend, but she is very tense. The boy is upset by her attitude towards his father. Her voice is described as 'mocking' and her face is 'blank' in his presence, yet she becomes very upset when the father and son leave.

Jim is the only character given a name. He is the mother's boyfriend. He is kind and interested in the boy but he is not his dad. He seems to feel sorry for the boy's father.

Form, Structure and Language

- **Symbolism** dominates the story. The title contains the most important symbols: the compass and the torch. A torch helps people to see things and a compass helps people find their way. They are both important objects on a trip like the one in the story. What do you think they mean in the context of the boy's relationship with his father? What is the significance of the compass being left behind?
- Do you think the wild ponies are also **symbolic**? What do they symbolise? This is an aspect of the story that can be read in different ways.
- The **imagery** used to describe nature gives a sense of mystery and danger: the rocks are like 'carcasses'; the ponies are 'ghost-coloured'.
- In contrast with the **vivid description** of the landscape, the conversations between characters are about everyday things in **colloquial** language. While the boy chatters on and asks questions, the man gives short, often monosyllabic, answers. The mother expresses herself quite violently, which is indicated by exclamation marks and question marks.
- The story is written in the **third person**. Sometimes the characters and settings are described as if seen from a distance. More often, the narrator takes us into the boy's thoughts, so that we see things from his point of view. Towards the end we get glimpses of the father's thoughts and feelings.
- The story is divided into short sections by **asterisks or dots**, which separate the different stages in the journey – a bit like scenes in a film.
- Most of the story is written in the **present tense**, although there are three short sections in the **past tense**, as the boy remembers what happened before he set off in the car with his father. Unusually, the final sentence uses the **future tense**, the writer predicting what will happen in the future.

When the Wasps Drowned Clare Wigfall

The Author

Clare Wigfall was born in Greenwich, London, in 1976 and grew up in Berkeley, California. She studied Creative Writing at Manchester University and travelled widely, living in Morocco, Spain and Norwich before settling in Prague. Her stories have been published in magazines and broadcast on Radio 4. This story was part of her first collection of short stories, published in 2007.

Narrative

During the summer holidays Eveline has to look after her younger brother and sister while her mother is at work. She is washing up the breakfast dishes when she hears a scream from the garden and sees her sister, Therese, running round the garden chased by wasps. Eveline runs outside and turns the hose on them. Therese has stood on a wasps' nest.

For the rest of the summer their mother makes them wear flip-flops. Sometimes they go to the park, but on other days they lie in the garden. Eveline sunbathes while Therese, watched by their brother Tyler, picks the dead wasps out of the grass.

Early in August Therese and Tyler start to dig a hole under the wall between their garden and Mr Mordecai's, saying that they are digging their way to Australia. Some time later, Eveline notices a ring on her sister's hand. When she asks her where she got it, Therese says she found it and takes her to the hole under the wall. Eveline reaches in and feels something. She sends her sister for a torch. The light shines on a dead hand. The children fill up the hole and Eveline takes the ring.

One day, when the holidays are over, two police officers call at the house and question the children about a girl who has disappeared. Shown a photograph and asked whether they recognise her, they all shake their heads. The police officers then go to Mr Mordecai's house. The children go into the garden.

Ideas, Themes and Issues

- **Family relationships**: the children are close, but both parents are absent – one permanently, one temporarily. The mother is always tired and, even when she is in, Eveline cooks for the family. None of the children tells her what has happened.
- **Death**: the dead wasps fascinate Therese as she picks them out of the grass. The other children just watch. Perhaps she is too young to have strong feelings about death. However, Eveline appears equally indifferent to the death of the young woman.
- **Growing up / Change**: Eveline, the narrator, is forced to grow up. She has to take care of her brother and sister and she takes charge when the body is found.
- **Innocence**: is this the end of innocence for the children? They seem happy and free in the garden, but after they find the body things surely can never be the same. But, apart from Therese's nightmares, we are not told how they react.
- **Honesty and responsibility**: Eveline chooses to keep the ring and lie to the police. There is no consideration of right and wrong. She takes responsibility for the children, but she does not feel any responsibility to the wider community. It does not occur to her to report that she has found a dead body. Is she putting the children first, is she worried about taking the ring or is she just not bothered?

Setting

The story is set mainly in the family's house and garden. The setting is not described in any detail. The only other setting is the local park. The house could be anywhere.

The story is set some time ago, in the summer. It could be the famously hot summer of 1976. Details in the story (such as transistor radios) support the idea that it might be set around this time.

Characters

Eveline's age is not given, but she is probably in her early teens. She is starting to grow up, making herself a bikini and showing interest in boys, but she still goes to bed early. She takes on the role of a mother, looking after the younger children. Although she is the narrator, we do not learn much about her feelings and emotions at the time or about what she, as an adult, might think about what happened.

Therese is younger than Eveline. She is frightened by the wasps when they attack her, but fascinated by them when they are dead. She is more active than the others, taking the lead in digging the tunnel. She does not show much emotion when she finds the body. However, she has nightmares about it.

Tyler, the youngest child, just seems to watch the others or follow their lead. We do not know if he has seen the body. Like Therese, he is dependent on Eveline, clinging to her when the police come.

Mum must be a single parent, but nothing is said about the children's father. She wears a uniform for work, so she could be anything from a nurse to a waitress. She seems to be tired all the time. Her absence is more important than her presence, as she knows nothing of what the children have found.

Mr Mordecai is never seen and has no contact with the children. The body is in his garden. Is he a murderer?

Form, Structure and Language

- The story is written in the **first person**. The narrator, Eveline, is looking back on an event from her childhood.
- There is not much descriptive detail in the story. Wigfall's style has been described as 'sparse'.
- There is, however, a lot of **symbolism** in the story. The garden represents an idyllic, innocent place, like the Garden of Eden in the Bible, but the episode with the wasps shows us that it is full of danger. Later we learn that death, in the form of the young woman's body, lies beneath it. What is the significance of the children going back into the garden at the end of the story?
- There is a **neutral tone** as the narrator simply tells us what happened without comment. We are left unaware of how she feels or what effect the events of the story have had on her. Some readers find this unsatisfying. Others think it creates a **chilling mood**. There is something odd and a bit frightening about Eveline's coolness.

My Polish Teacher's Tie Helen Dunmore

The Author

Helen Dunmore was born in Yorkshire in 1952. She had her first success as a poet but moved on to short stories and then novels. She has worked all over the world and says that her experience of different cultures and countries has been important for her work.

Narrative

Carla is a dinner lady in a school. One of her jobs is to serve tea and buns to the teachers in the staff room at break. During one break, the head announces that several Polish teachers are looking for pen friends in English schools, with a view to arranging an exchange visit.

Because Carla is half Polish, although she has forgotten all the Polish she ever knew, she is interested and asks for an address to write to. She exchanges letters with a teacher called Stefan, who asks to be called Steve. She tells him about her background and her family, but does not say anything about her job. In return, he sends her poems.

Some time later Carla is surprised to hear that Steve is coming to England and will be staying with one of the teachers, Mrs Kenward. She is worried he might feel hurt that she has not invited him to stay with her and that he will assume she is a teacher.

Mrs Kenward makes a lot of fuss about having Steve to stay and, when he arrives, says she finds him 'hard work'. Carla notices Steve sitting in the staff room. He is wearing a very wide, brightly coloured tie. She introduces herself to him. He smiles and sings a Polish song to her. It is one of the songs her mother used to sing and she finds herself joining in, remembering the words.

Ideas, Themes and Issues

- **Identity / Culture**: Carla is aware of her Polish background but she has lost touch with it. Steve helps her find a part of herself that was missing.
- **Poetry and song**: Steve is enthusiastic about poetry and songs. This shows how different he is from the English teachers – open, spontaneous and emotional.
- **Class / Status**: Carla is conscious that she is ignored by some teachers and looked down on by others. She feels defined by her uniform, but Steve – in spite of her worries – is not bothered about her status.

- **Relationships and family**: Carla appears to be a single parent with one daughter. She has been married (she is Mrs Carter) but we know nothing about her marriage or romantic history. When she writes to Steve she does not seem to be looking for a romantic relationship but we do not know if their friendship will turn into one.
- **Hopes and expectations**: Carla wants something more than a life pouring tea for teachers and takes a bold step in writing to Steve. Her expectations are low, but things turn out much better than she expects.

Setting

The main setting is the staff room of a school. It is not described in detail, and it would appear that the narrator does not feel the need to describe it. It is just part of her life – and for the staff she is possibly 'part of the furniture'. The staff room can be seen as a confined, conventional place where people are petty and unimaginative.

Characters

Carla does not go into detail about herself. She has a daughter and works as a dinner lady. The focus of the story is her 'lost' Polish background, which she rediscovers. She feels defined by her job and wants to break out. Although she worries what people might think about her, she is quite bold, first in asking for the address and later in going up to Steve and introducing herself.

Steve's real name is Stefan but he adopts the English form of his name, reflecting his love of English and his profession. He writes poetry. When he arrives at the school he gets a mixed response, but Carla is attracted to his eccentric dress sense and he shows himself to be spontaneous and without snobbery.

The teachers do not take much notice of Carla, although she knows their names and listens to their conversations. **Mrs Kenward**, at whose house Steve stays, is almost the opposite of him: critical, narrow-minded and with no love of poetry.

Form, Structure and Language

- The story is written in the **first person**, with Carla as the narrator.
- It starts in the **present tense**, with Carla telling us something about herself, but moves to the past as she tells the story. This makes it sound like she is chatting to us.
- The language is **chatty and colloquial**.
- The **tone** of the story is quite light-hearted and positive.
- Carla uses **similes** to describe her reaction, such as 'tense as a guitar string'. They are quite common similes, the sort people use in everyday conversation.

- **Letters** from Steve are quoted. In this way the reader hears his voice and point of view, just as Carla does.
- The English in Steve's letters is rather stilted and formal, as might be expected from someone who has learned English abroad.
- Steve's tie becomes a **symbol** of his unconventionality and his positive attitude: 'A flag from another country, a better country than the ones either of us lived in.'

Preparation Task

When you are re-reading the stories for revision, try making a 'storyboard' for each one. This will help you to identify the main points of the story and clarify the order in which things happen.

The Darkness Out There Penelope Lively

The Author

Penelope Lively was born in 1933 in Cairo. She has lived in England since being sent to boarding school at the age of 12. She became famous as a children's author before becoming equally successful as a writer of novels and stories for adults. She writes about memory and the relationship between the past and the present.

Narrative

A teenage girl, Sandra, goes to see an old lady called Mrs Rutter as part of her voluntary work for the Good Neighbours Club. Mrs Rutter lives in an isolated cottage near Packer's End, a spinney (small wood), which local people avoid. As she passes the spinney, Sandra meets a boy, Kerry. He is to be her 'partner' in the visit.

Mrs Rutter is very welcoming, asking them about themselves before giving them jobs to do: Kerry in the garden and Sandra in the house. Afterwards, she tells them what happened at Packer's End during the war.

Mrs Rutter's husband was killed in the war and she lived with her sister, Dot, in the cottage. One night in 1942, a plane crashed in the spinney. Because they did not have a telephone and the weather was bad, they went out to investigate before calling for help. When they got to the plane they saw that it was German, which pleased them. Two of the men inside were dead but one was still talking. Dot said he would not last long and they decided to leave him there.

The next day, the man was still alive, but Mrs Rutter decided not to do anything to help. The morning after, he was dead so she went to the village to inform the authorities. People came looking for souvenirs.

Kerry is shocked by what he has heard and leaves. Sandra follows.

Ideas, Themes and Issues

- **Growing up / Change**: Sandra and Kerry are both looking forward confidently to when they leave school and get jobs. Mrs Rutter's story makes them realise that there is a dark side to life.
- **Appearance and reality**: Mrs Rutter appears to be a stereotypical nice old lady, but her story reveals another side to her.
- **The past**: we can never escape the past.
- **Moral responsibility**: the Good Neighbours Club is all about helping people. But who are our neighbours? Should Mrs Rutter have helped the German or did the fact that he was 'the enemy' make a difference?

Setting

Although the story is set in the present day, the important events are in the past, during the Second World War. The contrast between life for young people now and then is important. Sandra and Kerry lead quite innocent, carefree lives, looking forward to a settled future. Things were very different for young people during the war.

The setting is like the setting for a fairytale. Going out into the country, Sandra is worried about what might be lurking in the woods. It is a dark place, in contrast to the open fields she walks through. Mrs Rutter's cottage is cosy and welcoming, making it an unlikely setting for her tale.

Characters

Sandra is an 'average' teenage girl. She comes from a secure background, likes sewing and looks forward to

falling in love. She expects to be a secretary when she leaves school. She has joined the Good Neighbours Club to help people and also to have fun with her friends. The story is seen mainly through her eyes. At the start of the story she is quite innocent and also quick to judge people but, disturbed by what she has heard, she has grown up a little by the end.

Kerry is just as 'ordinary'. He wants to leave school and become a mechanic. He is not especially popular and Sandra is not happy to be working with him. He is practical and works hard for the old lady. At the end, it is Kerry who is disturbed by Mrs Rutter's story and he who decides to leave, horrified by what happened to the German. Sandra feels that he has grown.

Mrs Rutter seems to be a typical old lady, housebound and in need of help. She is friendly and chatty, interested in Sandra and Kerry. When she tells her story we learn about her life when she was younger. Widowed in the war, her attitude to the Germans was typical. Her decision not to get help for the young man in the plane seems perfectly natural and right to her. Years later, it looks different to Kerry and Sandra and makes them see her in a different light.

Form, Structure and Language

- Packer's End is dark and mysterious. It is **symbolic**, representing 'the darkness out there'. What is the darkness?
- Sandra remembers thinking Packer's End would be full of witches and wolves, like in a **fairytale**. The story contains a lot of elements of a fairytale: not just the dark wood, but the girl setting off on her own, the cottage in the woods and the old lady. Which fairytales does it remind you of?
- It is written in the **third person**, but is seen mainly through Sandra's eyes. We know what she knows and we see what she sees.
- Mrs Rutter tells a story within a story. She does not do this as a continuous **narrative**, but is interrupted by questions and comments from the teenagers.
- There is a lot of **dialogue**, the **colloquial** language used adding to the ordinariness of the setting, in **contrast** to the horror of the story being told.
- In fact, the language of the whole narrative is colloquial and down to earth, as if we are sharing Sandra's thoughts.

On Seeing the 100% Perfect Girl… Haruki Murakami

The Author

Haruki Murakami was born in Japan in 1949. He is the son of two teachers of Japanese Literature, but from childhood has been influenced by American and other Western writers. After studying drama, he worked in a record shop and, with his wife, opened a coffee house and jazz bar. He is now one of Japan's most successful novelists. His work is humorous and surreal and is often concerned with loneliness. As well as writing, he competes in marathons and triathlons.

Narrative

The full title of the story is 'On Seeing the 100% Perfect Girl One Beautiful April Morning'.

One morning, in Tokyo, the narrator sees a girl who is perfect. He wishes he could speak to her and thinks of what he could say to her, but everything sounds ridiculous. When he passes her in front of a flower shop, he says nothing and she disappears.

He says that now he knows what he should have said. He should have told her a story starting with 'Once upon a time' and ended with a sad story.

He tells the story of a boy and girl who met when they were 18 and 16 and knew they were 100% perfect for each other. However, they began to have doubts and wondered if their dreams had come true too easily. The boy thought that if they really were perfect partners they could part and would meet again one day and marry. One winter they both caught flu and, although they recovered, they lost their memories. They became capable people and even fell in love with others, though only up to 75% or 85%. At last, when he was 32 and she was 30, they met on the street in Tokyo. For a moment they remembered, but the memories faded and they walked past each other.

That is the story he should have told the girl.

Ideas, Themes and Issues

- **City life**: life in Tokyo is busy, fast moving and exciting for some. However, the narrator of this story does not seem to find it so. Murakami is critical of the alienation people feel in modern cities – a sense of not belonging and being detached from life. People pass each other in the street but do not communicate.
- **Loneliness**: the narrator longs for someone to love. In his story he refers to himself as 'ordinary' and 'lonely' and imagines that the girl is also 'ordinary' and 'lonely'.
- **Love**: the narrator is a romantic. He wants to fall in love and imagines a perfect relationship.
- **Fantasy and reality**: the relationship remains a fantasy. In the story he makes up it is like a fairytale, but in real life he cannot bring himself even to speak to her. Even though he thinks she is 100% perfect when he sees her, the next day he cannot remember anything about her.
- **Time**: although he is only 32, the narrator is aware that he is growing older and that time is passing quickly.

Setting

The story is set in Tokyo's fashionable Haruyuku neighbourhood in April 1981. The time and place are very precise. Spring is traditionally a time of hope and renewal, a time when people might think about falling in love.

The city of Tokyo has a population of 8 million people, and is at the centre of the largest conurbation in the world, with a population of over 35 million people.

Haruyuku is a district where young people go to shop and relax, said to be a mixture of Japanese, 'American cool' and 'British rebellious' cultures. It could be a place where a young man might hope to meet a woman, but its crowded streets and lively atmosphere form a sharp contrast with the narrator's loneliness.

Characters

The **narrator** is 32, but feels that he is growing older. We do not know what he does for a living or anything about his family or friends, if he has any. Apart from the girl, the only person he mentions is referred to as 'someone'. He describes himself as 'lonely'.

We know nothing about **the girl** except for what the boy sees. She is about 30 and, according to him, not a great beauty. Indeed, he can hardly remember anything about her. However, in his fantasy she is just like him: lonely and looking for love.

Form, Structure and Language

- The story can be divided into five parts:
  1. The story opens in the past tense, with the narrator addressing the reader.
  2. He then switches to the present tense as he describes a conversation with someone else.
  3. Now he describes the meeting; although he spoke about it in the past tense before, he still uses the present tense.
  4. Then, using the past tense, he tells the story that he wishes he had told the girl in the street.
  5. Finally, in the last two lines, he addresses the reader again.
- Why do you think the narrator changes **tenses** when he does?
- The fourth section is a 'story within a story'. Its style is quite different from the rest of the story. Its use of the **past tense**, its **simple sentences** and phrases such as 'once upon a time' are reminiscent of a **fairytale** or **legend**.
- In the fourth section the narrator uses the **third person**, distancing himself from the boy in the story.
- The **first person narrative** in the rest of the story is **informal** and **conversational** in **tone**, as the narrator addresses the reader directly as 'you'.
- Although the story takes place in Japan, there are references to **Western culture**, such as Woody Allen and D.H. Lawrence.
- The letter that the girl is carrying and the flower shop outside which he meets her are important **symbols**. What do they make the reader think about?

Something Old, Something New Leila Aboulela

The Author

Leila Aboulela was born in 1964 in Egypt and grew up in Khartoum, Sudan. She moved to Scotland and started writing and being published whist looking after her family in Aberdeen. She says that her faith is central to her life and to her writing.

Narrative

A young Scotsman arrives in Khartoum. He is met by his fiancée, a Sudanese woman, and her brother, and taken to the Hilton Hotel, where he is to stay until they marry. She tells him that she will need an exit visa to leave the country with him.

They met in a restaurant in Edinburgh, where she was a waitress, after Friday night prayers at the local mosque. He had converted to Islam after dropping out of university. She had been brought to Edinburgh by her husband from whom she was now divorced.

In Sudan, the man meets his fiancée's family and enjoys outings, always accompanied by members of the family. One day his passport and camera are stolen. He is angry, but she is embarrassed by his reaction. After visiting the British embassy, she in turn becomes angry at their attitude. When they return to the family house they learn that her uncle has died and three days of mourning follow. The man is not allowed to see his fiancée and the wedding plans are in jeopardy.

After the mourning period they get married in a simple ceremony at her brother's flat. At last they are alone together.

Ideas, Themes and Issues

- **Religion and faith**: both characters are Muslims, although the man has converted from Christianity. At first, she finds it odd that a white man should be a Muslim, as does the Imam who marries them. The relationship between religion, culture and background is explored. He feels that Islam has allowed him to ask big questions. He says he already believed in God and was brought up as a Catholic. In contrast with her attitude to Islam, the author seems almost to dismiss his religious background. Do you think this is a weakness in the story?
- **Cultural differences**: it is interesting that the story is written from the Scotsman's point of view rather than the Sudanese woman's. He is eager to embrace her culture but there are aspects of it he finds surprising and perhaps disturbing.
- **Love and marriage**: this is a love story. Two people from different backgrounds fall in love and overcome obstacles and misunderstandings to get married. The woman previously had an arranged marriage, which failed, although she loved her husband.
- **Family**: the closeness of her family is strange to the man, but it is something that the death of her uncle causes him to appreciate.
- **Society**: generally Sudanese society is seen in a positive light, but there is violence and greed. Scottish society is seen as being undermined by drugs.

Setting

The story is set mainly in Sudan, the largest country in Africa. Sudan has had a long history of political instability, with conflict between the mainly Muslim north and the mainly Christian south. In recent years, the southern region of Darfur has been the centre of a humanitarian crisis caused by the ongoing civil war. This is only very briefly referred to in the story, which takes place in the capital, Khartoum, in the north.

The city is described from the point of view of the man as a mixture of the familiar and the exotic: the luxurious hotel that he stays in; tourist destinations like the camel market; the Blue Nile. He also recalls how he met the woman in Edinburgh. The Scottish city is very different with its green and grey houses, the castle and Arthur's seat, yet his experience of being shown round Khartoum is similar to hers of being shown round Edinburgh.

Religion, specifically Islam, is central. He hears the 'azan' or call to prayer. The funeral ceremony and wedding ceremony are described in detail. In addition, both dress and food are unfamiliar to the protagonist. People speak in Arabic, which he knows only as the language of religion.

Characters

The man is described as always being top of his class until he went to university and started to drift. Converting to Islam has given him a new purpose in life and helped him to settle down. He is eager to please his fiancée and her family, but becomes angry when things go wrong. At the end he admits he has found his experience 'rough'.

The woman went to Scotland to marry, but divorced after six months because of her husband's infidelity. She is seen mainly through the man's eyes as beautiful and calm, but he is upset when he thinks she is laughing at him. She, in turn, gets angry, after visiting the embassy to ask for a visa. When he asks her, at the end, if she feels sorry for him she says she does. Why?

The woman's family is very close. **Her brother** is very protective, but he is also a little threatening and is always keen to take money. However, the two men seem to gain an understanding of each other before the wedding. **Her uncle** is seen as an amusing character at first but, when he dies, he comes to symbolise the family's values. His death also causes problems for the wedding.

Form, Structure and Language

- The narrative is in the **third person**, but it is seen through the man's eyes.
- The title refers to the **traditional rhyme** about weddings. To what else might it refer?
- Quite a few **Arabic words and phrases** are used, especially about food and religion.
- References are made to **popular culture**: the uncle is compared to Bill Cosby and the family to the Mafia family in *The Godfather*.
- There is a lot of **direct speech**, telling us about the characters and their attitudes.
- The story is mainly a **chronological account** of a few days in Sudan, but with a short 'flashback' to the couple's meeting and courtship in Edinburgh.

Anil Ridjal Noor

The Author

Ridjal Noor was born in 1979 in Malaysia, but now lives in Singapore. As well as writing, he works as a graphic designer.

Narrative

In a remote village, a boy called Anil is awake in the middle of the night. He needs to go to the toilet but is frightened of going outside his family's hut in the dark. Looking out of the window, he hears a voice. It is someone calling 'Marimuthu'. He recognises the name as that of the village headman's brother. Outside, a man throws a rope over the branches of a large tree.

Marimuthu and the other man are hanging a woman from the tree. She is still alive and Anil watches her die.

In the morning, when both his parents have left, Anil goes outside and sees the noose still hanging from the tree, but no body. He sees his parents and the neighbours in a circle and pushes his way through them. The woman's body is on the ground, cradled by the headman's mother. The woman's husband is also there, wailing. The husband is Marimuthu. The headman announces that the woman must have committed suicide and says that there is no need to report this to the authorities. Anil tells Marimuthu and the headman that he knows that Marimuthu killed her.

The headman takes Anil's father, Ragunathan, and Anil to his house to talk about Anil.

Later Ragunathan sees Anil off on a train. He tells him he will be successful and make his father proud. Anil asks if he is being sent away to school because he witnessed the murder. His father just says that someday he will understand. Anil vows that he will never forget what happened. Back in the village, the woman's body is burned.

Ideas, Themes and Issues

- **Childhood / Growing up**: Anil is only seven. He is frightened of the dark and of his father. However, he is old enough to understand what he has seen and innocently tells both the murderer and the headman. He has to grow up quickly, leaving his family at a very early age.
- **Family**: there are two families – Anil's and the headman's. Both the headman and Anil's father can be seen as bullies, and both put their families before moral principles.
- **Power**: the headman has great power in the village. He thinks he is above the law.
- **Rich and poor**: Anil's family and the rest of the villagers are very poor. They depend on the headman for employment. The headman can buy Ragunathan's silence.
- **Men and women**: the men are violent bullies, while the women are painted as victims. Ragunathan beats his wife; Marimuthu kills his.
- **Justice / Morality**: there is no justice in this society and only Anil seems concerned by the fact that a sin has been committed. The headman and his brother are too rich to be concerned about right and wrong, while Anil's father is too poor.

Setting

The story is set in a village in Malaysia, where people follow a traditional way of life. They are dependent on the land and on the headman of the village. Although the headman refers to 'the authorities' – presumably the police or other government agencies – they do not seem to have much influence.

The village is very poor, the people living in huts that let in the rain, and dreaming of simple things like a good harvest or a new cow. We do not know exactly where Anil is going at the end of the story, but it is a world away from the rural society in which he has been brought up.

Characters

Anil is a typical seven-year-old boy, whose life is changed forever because of what he sees. He is frightened by what he sees, but he knows it is wrong and, innocently, tells the headman. He does not want to leave home but has no choice.

Amma (**mother**), is a poor woman, the victim of her husband's violence. She works for the headman. She does not seem to have any say in what happens to her son.

Ragunathan or **Appa** (**father**) is described as 'burly', and as a bully in relation to his family but a mouse in relation to the headman. He is the headman's servant and does as he is told. We do not know how he comes to the arrangement to send Anil away, but he tells his son it is a great opportunity and he will be grateful for it. However, our last glimpse of him is as a 'despaired' man.

Marimuthu is the headman's brother. We do not know why he has murdered his wife. The important thing is that he is allowed to get away with it.

The headman represents power and authority. He is corrupt and allows his brother to get away with murdering his wife. We do not discover whether he knew about the murder beforehand or whether he is just covering up out of loyalty to his brother.

Form, Structure and Language

- The narrative is in the **third person**, but – except for the final two paragraphs – is seen through the eyes of Anil.
- It is divided into **two sections**. The long first section describes the events of the night of the murder and the following day. The second section reveals the outcome of Ragunathan's visit to the headman's bungalow.
- The **opening** of the story is like that of a **folk tale** or **fairy tale**. Most of the writing is fairly simple, with a lot of short paragraphs.
- **Descriptive details** give a sense of place and the kind of life the villagers lead: Amma wears a faded sari; there are pots under the roof to catch the rain.
- There is **irony** in the outcome of the story. Anil is the only character to know that what has happened is wrong, but he is going to benefit from the crime.

Poetry

The study of poetry is a very important part of GCSE English Literature. Your knowledge and understanding of poetry can be tested in two ways and your teachers will have decided which way they prefer. You will study either:

- Unit 2: Poetry Across Time, or
- Unit 5: Exploring Poetry

Unit 2

If you are doing Unit 2, you will sit an examination with two parts. The first part contains questions about the poems in the anthology, *Moon on the Tides*, and the second part contains a question about a poem you have never seen before.

Unit 5

If you are doing Unit 5 you will be tested through controlled assessment. Your teachers have a free choice of which poems to use to prepare you for the assessment but many of them will choose to teach poetry from the anthology.

Poems in the Anthology

The anthology contains a total of 60 poems, but don't worry – you will not be expected to study all of them! The poems are divided into four 'clusters':

- Cluster 1: Character and Voice
- Cluster 2: Place
- Cluster 3: Conflict
- Cluster 4: Relationships

For the exam you will study one 'cluster' of 15 poems. Eight of these are 'contemporary' poems, written by living poets. The other seven are from the 'English Literary Heritage' and were written by poets who wrote as long ago as the seventeenth century, or as recently as the twentieth.

This book discusses each poem individually as well as giving a brief introduction to each cluster. In the exam you will have to compare two poems – and in the controlled assessment you will have to study a group of poems – so make sure that when you study a poem, you try to make connections with other poems in the cluster, looking at differences as well as similarities.

The overview of each poem on the following pages is divided into four sections: **content**; how the poem fits into the cluster; **ideas, themes and issues**; and **form, structure and language**. Some information about the poet is also given.

Content: Think about what happens in the poem. Some of these poems tell a story, while others are about a person's thoughts or feelings. When commenting on a poem, you need to show that you have understood what is going on, but avoid simply re-telling the story.

Ideas, Themes and Issues: This really means 'what the poem is about'. The title of each cluster gives you a clue about what some of the main themes are, but you will also find that many of the poems touch on other themes and ideas. You might find that a poet's attitude is very clear, but sometimes it might be ambiguous or you will have to make up your own mind about the ideas and issues in the poem.

Form, Structure and Language: Form and structure refer to how the poem is arranged and set out, for example, whether it is arranged in stanzas, whether the lines are of equal length, whether there is a regular metre or rhythm or whether there is a rhyme scheme. Language is about the words the poets use, not only the choice of vocabulary but also the sound of the words and the pictures they create through imagery.

You may come across words used to describe form, structure and language that you have not seen before. If you are unsure of their meaning, look them up in the Glossary of Literary Terms on pages 85–86.

Cluster 1: Character and Voice

Each of the 15 poems in Cluster 1 focuses on one character, but there are many different approaches to writing about a character. In the exam you will have to make connections between poems, looking at differences and similarities between the characters presented, and differences and similarities between the ways in which the poets present their characters.

Many of the poems are written in the **first person** ('I'), but in some of them the 'I' is the voice of the poet, while in others the poet adopts a **persona** – in other words, the poet takes on the role of the character and writes as if he / she actually is that person.

Sometimes when the poets write as themselves, they are observers in the poems, describing characters that they may have known (e.g. *On a Portrait of a Deaf Man*) or have simply seen and wondered about (e.g. *The Hunchback in the Park*). Other poets write about their own feelings and experiences (e.g. *Checking Out Me History*).

When writing as characters, poets might write as if they were thinking about their lives or explaining themselves to an unnamed listener. The poem might even take the form of a conversation between two characters, as in *The Ruined Maid*.

You will meet a wide range of characters in these poems, from a 16th-century Italian Duke (*My Last Duchess*) to a mythical monster (*Medusa*) and from an old tramp (*The Hunchback in the Park*) to a young girl's imaginary friend (*Brendon Gallacher*).

By writing about these people the poets are able to explore a wide variety of ideas, themes and issues. Here are just some of the common themes touched upon in this cluster:

- **Identity and culture**: *Checking Out Me History*, *Horse Whisperer*, *Singh Song!*.
- **Power**: *The River God*, *My Last Duchess*, *Ozymandias*, *Medusa*, *Horse Whisperer*.
- **Men and women**: *Medusa*, *My Last Duchess*, *The Ruined Maid*, *Singh Song!*.
- **Ordinary lives**: *The Ruined Maid*, *On a Portrait of a Deaf Man*, *The Hunchback In the Park*, *Give*, *Singh Song!*.
- **Outsiders**: *Checking Out Me History*, *The Hunchback in the Park*, *The Ruined Maid*, *On a Portrait of a Deaf Man*, *Give*, *Horse Whisperer*.
- **Childhood**: *Brendon Gallacher*, *The Hunchback in the Park*, *Checking Out Me History*.
- **Death and mortality**: *Ozymandias*, *The River God*, *My Last Duchess*, *On a Portrait of a Deaf Man*, *Casehistory*: *Alison (head injury)*.

Helpful Hint

Remember, responding to poetry is not just about 'translating' or 'decoding' a poem's meaning. It is just as much about what the poem makes *you* think and how it makes *you* feel. How do you respond to the people in these poems? Have you ever felt the way they feel?

The Clown Punk Simon Armitage

The Poet

Simon Armitage was born in Huddersfield, Yorkshire. After studying in Portsmouth and Manchester he worked as, among other things, a probation officer and a DJ before becoming a writer. He still lives in Yorkshire. Many of his poems contain references to aspects of life in the North of England, as well as to his own family background.

Content

The poem describes a local character, a man who dresses like a punk and walks round with a dog on the end of a rope. He is covered in tattoos.

As he crosses the road, he presses his face against the car's windscreen, making the children in the back scream. The poet asks the children to think about what the 'clown punk' will look like in 30 years' time.

Character and Voice

The voice is the voice of the poet. He could be anyone driving home through town, with his children in the back of the car. He describes a well-known local figure. He does not give the man a voice or give any details about his character and feelings apart from what he sees in a brief encounter.

According to Armitage, this poem is based on a real event. When he stopped at traffic lights the man he describes pressed his face against the windscreen. He does not know what has happened to the 'clown punk'.

Ideas, Themes and Issues

- **The outsider and society**: the 'clown punk' is on the edge of the town's society. He is seen in the rough part of town, he dresses oddly and he acts oddly. The poet and his family, in contrast, are secure and conventional in their car.
- **Strangers / Chance meetings**: in an interview, Armitage has referred to a tradition in poetry where poets write about chance encounters. He speaks of something passing between strangers. He feels empathy for the stranger, although he knows nothing about him.
- **Time**: he asks his children to think about the future of the clown punk. He speculates on what he will look like when he is old. What was once fashionable, and is now a bit frightening, might look ridiculous and pathetic.

Form, Structure and Language

- The poem is written in the **first person**. The poet is part of the poem.
- At first he addresses the reader or anyone who might drive through his home town. He seems to be giving us advice, or a warning, about the character.
- Later he addresses his children – or any children who might react to the clown punk.
- At the start and end of the poem he uses **rhyme** (town / clown), **half rhyme** (scream / windscreen) and **internal rhyme** (town / clown), together with quite a **strong rhythm**, creating a **playful, almost childish tone**.
- However, in the middle section (the second stanza and the first half of the third) the **rhythm** breaks down; the **tone is more thoughtful** and a little sad.
- The car could be seen as a **symbol** of modern society: the clown punk is outside it and attacks it.
- The final **rhyming couplet** gives a neat ending to the poem, but leaves us with the image of the punk and the rain on the windscreen, symbolising the passing of time.

Checking Out Me History John Agard

The Poet

John Agard was born in British Guiana (now Guyana) in the West Indies in 1949. He moved to Britain in 1977 and has written many poems about his struggle to find a sense of identity as a man of mixed race.

Content

The poet talks about what he was taught at school: British history and stories. He was not told the stories of men and women from the West Indies. Now he is finding out for himself about his history.

Character and Voice

Agard is writing in his own voice about his own experiences, although they would be the experiences of many others from similar backgrounds. As part of his assertion of his identity, he rejects Standard English and writes in the dialect of his region.

In the poem he tells the stories of three characters from history: Toussaint L'Ouverture, Nanny Maroon and Mary Seacole. These were West Indians, whose achievements would have been ignored in the schools of Agard's youth, where a British curriculum was taught, but are now generally regarded as heroes in the West Indies.

Ideas, Themes and Issues

- **Identity**: at the end of the poem Agard says he is 'carving out me identity'. He feels that people like him have been ignored and their experiences denied so he needs to make his own identity.
- **History**: history is important in shaping people's sense of themselves. By being taught history that had no relevance to him, the poet was made to feel inferior and oppressed. Now he is rediscovering the history of his own people.
- **Education**: the kind of education he received is seen as a tool of the British Empire to oppress people like him and leave them feeling inferior. Now he is educating himself in a way that makes him feel positive and proud.

Form, Structure and Language

- He writes the way he would speak, using 'dem' for 'them' and using the present tense throughout (e.g. 'travel' instead of 'travelled'). The way he expresses himself is important. His rejection of **Standard English** is an act of rebellion.
- There is a lot of **repetition**, giving a sense of the message being hammered home by his teachers.
- When he describes what he was taught he uses **regular four line stanzas**, usually **rhyming** all four lines. This and the **simple vocabulary** give a rather childish sing-song effect, which is appropriate to the subject.
- The longer stanzas which alternate with these, describing his heroes, also **rhyme** but they are not as regular and so there is a sense of freedom – breaking out of the simple pattern of his childhood.
- He uses very positive **visual imagery** of fire and light to describe his heroes: Touissant is a 'beacon', Nanny a 'fire-woman', and Mary Seacole a 'yellow sunrise'.

Helpful Hint

To help you understand the importance of sound in a poem, read it aloud or listen to someone else reading it. You might get the chance to hear some of the anthology poetry read by the poets themselves at a live event. You can also access recordings of poets reading their work on the internet, for example, on The Poetry Archive site.

Horse Whisperer Andrew Forster

The Poet

Andrew Forster grew up in South Yorkshire but now lives in Scotland, where he works as a Literature Development Officer. His first collection of poetry was published in 2007. He draws on his own experience, with poems based on his childhood, but also writes about real and imagined figures from the past.

Content

The 'horse whisperer' tells the story of how he used to be in demand, needed by people who were having trouble with their horses. However, when horses were no longer needed for farm work he fell from favour and his skills were condemned as witchcraft. He used his knowledge to take his revenge before emigrating. Looking back, he misses the horses he worked with.

Character and Voice

A 'horse whisperer' is someone who trains horses without using violence or force. The term has become popular as a result of a film based on the work of a well-known American horse whisperer.

There is nothing mysterious or magical about the methods of real horse whisperers. Their work is based on equine psychology, involving gentle persuasion and an understanding of how horses relate to each other. The whisperer in this poem, however, uses 'charms' to control the horses. It could be this that leads people to think that he is a witch and has no place in the modern world.

He looks back on his life and sees his work as a thing of the past, but he is proud of what he has achieved.

Ideas, Themes and Issues

- **The past / History**: the world has moved on and left the horse whisperer behind. His skills are no longer useful. There is a tone of regret at the loss of ancient skills and of old communities. The speaker is conscious that he is part of a tradition.
- **Man and nature**: in the past people and animals had a close relationship, working together on farms. In a more mechanical age we have lost the ability to communicate with nature.
- **Work**: the horse whisperer takes pride in his work. When he describes his emigration he identifies himself with others whose 'trades' are no longer necessary. Having a trade gives people a sense of identity and worth.
- **Religion and superstition**: the horse whisperer is denounced from pulpits as a witch. This makes him act like a witch, putting curses on people. It is not clear whether he believes his skills are magical.

Form, Structure and Language

- The poem is written in the **first person**, with the poet adopting the **persona** of someone from another time and place.
- The poem consists of five **stanzas**, each one shorter than the last. This might give a sense of the character fading away through history.
- The first four stanzas are in the past tense as the horse whisperer looks back on his life. The final stanza, in the present tense, sums up his feelings about his past. The tone is both nostalgic and proud.
- The language used to describe horses is strong and vigorous.
- The horses are closely associated with the man: the man joins a 'stampede' of emigrants; at the end he speaks of 'pride', referring both to the horses and himself.

Medusa Carol Ann Duffy

The Poet

Carol Ann Duffy was born in Glasgow in 1955. She is often seen as a feminist poet, writing about women's experiences. In 2009 she became Britain's first female Poet Laureate.

Content

A woman tells her lover that she is worried that he will leave her now that she is old and ugly. She says it would be better if he were stone.

Character and Voice

In ancient Greek mythology, Medusa was a beautiful woman, who was raped in the Temple of Athene by Poseidon, the god of the sea. Athene then turned Medusa's hair into snakes and made her unable to look

at anything without turning it into stone. The hero, Perseus, killed her by using his shield as a mirror while he cut off her head.

Duffy uses some aspects of the Greek myth in creating her character, but her experience does not always reflect the Medusa myth.

Here, the voice is that of a woman who is getting old and is worried that her lover will leave her. After she mentions 'stone', she takes on the role of Medusa, while the man being addressed becomes Perseus.

Ideas, Themes and Issues

- **Men and women**: the poem does not refer to Poseidon, but implies that 'Medusa' was responsible for the changes in herself. Were her suspicion, doubt and jealousy justified? Or does our knowledge of the Medusa myth lead us to think it is all men's fault? Either way, her relationship with men could be seen as the root of her problems.
- **Age**: she looks back wistfully at her youth and her beauty. She has changed from a beautiful woman to a monster. Is Duffy saying that this happens to all women? Or that, in a world where women are judged by their looks, this is how they are made to feel?
- **Love and desire**: the woman says that she loves the man she is addressing, but she cannot keep him. She would rather he turned to stone than left her. However, the last stanza implies that he will destroy her (rather than her destroying him), as Perseus destroyed Medusa.

Form, Structure and Language

- The use of a **persona** is especially interesting in this poem as the speaker seems to become Medusa part way through.
- There are seven **stanzas**, of equal length, each consisting of six lines, followed by one of a single line. The first three are in the **present tense** and the next three in the **past tense** before the seventh returns to the **present**. Why might this be?
- The three-word final line is very powerful. Why?
- The myth of Medusa is used as an **extended metaphor**, perhaps for the experience of all women.
- She uses the myth to create **vivid imagery**, e.g. the shield and the dragon, but also uses images from ordinary everyday life. This woman is both an ordinary woman and a creature of myth.

Singh Song! Daljit Nagra

The Poet

Daljit Nagra was born in 1966 and brought up in London, where he teaches English. His family came from the Punjab, India. He says he is 'obsessed with Asian-ness', writing about the experiences of Asian people in Britain.

Content

The character (persona) of the poem talks about his daily life. He runs one of his father's shops and has recently married. He should work from 9 in the morning until 9 at night, but when there are no customers he locks up and goes upstairs to his wife. At night they both go down into the shop and look out at the moonlit view.

Character and Voice

Nagra assumes the voice of a Sikh shopkeeper. The title is a pun on the common Sikh surname, Singh, and 'sing song', an expression that is sometimes used to describe the rhythm of an Indian accent. His strong accent is conveyed in the unusual spelling in the poem.

The persona might be thought of as a stereotypical character, working all day without a break in the family shop. However, he defies his father by taking breaks and has married a rather unconventional woman, who has no respect for his parents. He is in love with his wife and, in spite of his unrewarding job, seems to be happy.

Ideas, Themes and Issues

- **Cultural identity**: the character's identity as a Punjabi Sikh is sharply drawn, from his accented English to references to typical Indian foods. The shopping precinct, the beaches and the shoppers are part of the English setting. He might be seen as an outsider, but he seems to be part of an established Asian community: 'di whole Indian road'. His wife's ethnic origin is not clear but her eccentric dress reflects a joyful fusion of cultures.
- **Family**: the character is fulfilling the stereotype of the loyal Indian son, working in his father's business, but he disobeys the rules and his wife's behaviour towards his parents is shockingly, but amusingly, lacking in respect.
- **Love**: the most important thing in his life is his new bride. He loves her unconventionality, and the idea that she is above him while he works in the shop. The last few lines, when they talk about the moon, are tender and romantic.

Form, Structure and Language

- Nagra conveys the way his character speaks by changing the spelling of words to reflect his **accent**, for example using 'vee' for 'we' and 'di' for 'the'.
- He also uses **non-standard grammar**: 'Di girls dat are pinching my sweeties'. This has a rather comic effect. It might remind you of how people talk when making fun of and exaggerating Indian accents.
- The poem is in the **present tense**, reflecting the fact that he is telling us about what he does every day.
- There is a lot of **repetition** ('my bride…'; 'from di stool'), adding to the sense of the daily routine.
- A voice is given to the customers as well as to the shopkeeper. Their complaints sound a bit like a **chorus** or **chant**, ending in the **repeated** two lines: 'in di worst Indian shop / on di whole Indian road.'
- He uses a lot of **rhyme** and **half-rhyme**, adding to the **humour** and the **song-like** quality of the poem.

Brendon Gallacher Jackie Kay

The Poet

Jackie Kay was born in Edinburgh to a Scottish mother and Nigerian father, and was adopted as a baby by a white couple. She has explored her heritage, her sense of identity and her experience of adoption in novels, plays and poetry.

Content

The poet tells us about her childhood friend, Brendon Gallacher. He came from a different kind of family from hers, but they would play together and talk about their families. The friendship lasted for two years before the girl's mother told her that a neighbour had said that there was nobody called Gallacher at the address where Brendon was supposed to live. Her friend was imaginary and from that moment he ceased to exist for her.

Character and Voice

The voice is that of the poet as an adult, looking back on herself at the age of six.

She tells us a little about her family: she was Scottish, she had one brother and her father worked for the Communist Party. She seems to come from quite a happy family and does not mention any problems, yet she is a solitary child, going out on her own and inventing a friend for company.

Brendon Gallacher, the child she invents, is appealing because he is so different from her. He is from a big Irish family, his father is in prison, his mother drinks and they are very poor.

Ideas, Themes and Issues

- **Childhood**: the poet looks back on an episode from her childhood, without commenting on what it means. There is a note of sadness as she recalls her imaginary friend.
- **Family**: the two families described are very different. Why does she invent an imaginary family so different from her own?
- **Imagination**: the child prefers the world of the imagination to the 'real' world. Perhaps she wants to escape to this world.
- **Heritage and Identity**: in inventing a new family, she might be 'trying out' a different identity. She defines the two families by class and nationality. She might feel that these two things shape identity and she is unsure where she really belongs.

Form, Structure and Language

- In each stanza all five lines **rhyme** or **half rhyme**. In fact, all the lines almost rhyme with the repeated name, 'Brendon Gallacher'. This both places emphasis on the name, stressing his importance, and makes the poem suitable for reading aloud – or even singing – reflecting the influence of the great Scottish poet, Robert Burns.
- The poem starts with a series of **contrasts**, showing the difference between the two children's backgrounds.
- The use of the **possessive pronouns** 'my' by the poet and 'your' by her mother are common when talking about someone's friend, but might also be a clue that Brendon 'belongs' to the girl and does not really have a life of his own.
- The language is **colloquial** and includes some Scots **dialect** words and expressions.
- Brendon becomes a **symbol** of the poet's childhood and when he 'dies' she loses something forever. The last line with the **repeated** 'Oh' is like a lament or expression of grief, helping to give the poem an **elegiac mood**.

Give Simon Armitage

The Poet

See page 22.

Content

A beggar on the street says that he has chosen this place to make a scene. He has chosen a particular doorway to sleep in. He says that he can do tricks for money. The listener gives him a cup of tea.

Character and Voice

Armitage adopts the persona of a beggar on the street. He is homeless and sleeps in doorways. He begs for change. For most of the poem he seems to be quite upbeat and entertaining, talking about sword swallowing and escapology. However, at the end, he is without hope.

The speaker is not given a background or any particular characteristics. We do not know who he (it could even be a she) is and how he (or she) came to be homeless. Armitage's beggar could, therefore, be representative of all beggars. Perhaps the lack of detail reflects how little notice most people take of beggars.

Ideas, Themes and Issues

- **The outsider**: the beggar is 'outside' normal society. He is an inconvenience or annoyance to the people he stops in the street.
- **Poverty**: the beggar has nothing. He represents a part of society that most people would prefer to forget. He will do more or less anything for money.
- **How we see others**: the beggar's voice is not normally heard. Here, he is given a chance to express his feelings about his life.
- **Responsibility**: the beggar cannot help himself, but perhaps we can and should help him and others in the same position.

Form, Structure and Language

- The beggar is speaking directly to someone addressed as 'dear'. Is this a particular person, someone he has known in the past, or just the person who happens to be passing? Perhaps the reader is being addressed. If so, why does he use the word 'dear'? Is it affectionate or patronising?
- The poet uses **rhyme** and a **regular rhythm** to give the poem an upbeat tone, making the beggar seem almost happy with his lot. The language used when he describes the tricks he can do reinforces this.
- However, there is a dramatic change of **tone** in the final stanza. The **broken lines** and **simple language** bring us down to earth.
- There are references to the Bible in line 10, and to films in line 3.
- Armitage uses **puns or double meanings**: to make a scene could mean having a public row or putting on a show, while 'change' in line 10 refers to both money and a change in his life.
- The final, direct plea of the last line underlines both his inability to help himself and the possibility of the listener or reader doing something to help.

Practice Question

Answer the following Foundation Tier question in 45 minutes. Answer both parts of the question.

Part (a) What sort of person is the poet writing about in 'Give'?

Part (b) Compare the ways in which the poets present characters in this poem and one other poem from 'Character and Voice'.

Les Grands Seigneurs Dorothy Molloy

The Poet

Dorothy Molloy was born in County Mayo in the west of Ireland and grew up near Dublin, where she studied Modern Languages at university. She later worked as an historical researcher in Barcelona, Spain. Her poetry reflects her interest in European languages and history. Her poems often focus on male–female relationships.

Content

A woman describes what men used to mean to her. They amused her and gave her pleasure. They loved and admired her, but she stayed out of their reach. But then she was married and things changed. Now she is the 'plaything' and her husband is in charge.

Character and Voice

The title and the references to courtly love suggest that the setting for the poem is France, probably in the Middle Ages. 'Les Grands Seigneurs' literally means 'the great lords' – men of high rank.

The speaker is a woman, probably also of high rank. She is attractive to men and attracted to them. She has enjoyed 'playing' at courtly love and having men try to impress her to gain her affection. Then she marries and her role changes.

Ideas, Themes and Issues

- **Men and women**: she speaks about men as pets or toys and herself as a queen, commanding them and playing with them. Later, the man is in charge. The relationship is never equal.
- **Courtly love**: a court in this sense refers to the home of a king and to the people who surround him and serve him. Male 'courtiers' would try to impress women by writing songs and poetry to them, while the women would pretend to resist and treat them cruelly. So, during courtship the women were in command, but once married, the man would be head of the household.
- **Appearance and reality**: is the whole idea of 'courtly love' a fantasy? Before her marriage, the woman is acting a role, but after marriage she discovers harsh reality. It is as if society has played a trick on her.
- **Love and desire**: the men want her but she is 'out of reach' until she is 'wedded and bedded'. There is no indication of whether she loves any of the men, whether they love her, or what love means.

Form, Structure and Language

- The poem is written in the **first person**, the poet adopting the **persona** of a woman from the distant past. Is she just writing about what happened a long time ago or does the poem say anything about men and women now?
- There are four **stanzas**. The first two describe what she thought of men. The third tells of her role and the fourth tells us about her life after marriage.
- The first three stanzas are rich in **imagery**. First, she uses **metaphors** that compare men to places. Then she compares them to various animals. These animals are tame and decorative.
- She uses **diction** that is appropriate to a woman of her class and is associated with the Middle Ages.
- The language changes dramatically from the third to the fourth stanzas. It becomes more modern and **colloquial**. The **images** that describe her as a wife are common images, which might be thought of as demeaning to women: 'plaything'; 'bit of fluff'.

Ozymandias Percy Bysshe Shelley

The Poet

Percy Bysshe Shelley (1792–1822) was one of a group of poets known as the Romantics. They wrote about nature and human emotions, as well as having radical political ideas. Shelley led an unconventional life with his second wife Mary, the author of *Frankenstein*. He drowned off the coast of Italy aged 29.

Content

The poet tells of a meeting with someone from 'an antique land', who described to him the remains of the statue of an ancient king which he has seen standing in the desert.

Character and Voice

Ozymandias was a Greek version of one of the names of Rameses ll, the ancient Egyptian pharoah. He may have been the pharaoh mentioned in the story of Moses in the Bible.

There are three voices in this poem. The poem begins in first person as the poet reports what the traveller said to him. This adds an air of mystery and distance to what the traveller describes. We learn nothing about the traveller himself; his only role is to tell the poet and us about the statue, its sculptor and the king. The king himself is given a voice when the traveller repeats the words inscribed on the base of the statue.

Ideas, Themes and Issues

- **Death and mortality**: all that survives of the great king are the remains of his statue – two legs, a pedestal and a 'shattered visage'. Whatever our position in life, death comes to all of us.
- **Power**: Ozymandias was 'king of kings'. His power was absolute and the face of the statue shows that he was cruel ('the sneer of cold command'). There is no sympathy for him.
- **Art**: the sculptor is described as having captured the reality of his subject. His art (although partly ruined) lives on long after the death of the king. Does this make an artist more powerful than a ruler?

Form, Structure and Language

- The poem is in the form of a **sonnet**. It has fourteen lines and is written in **iambic pentameter**. Traditionally, sonnets were love poems, but Shelley used them to explore political ideas.
- Traditional Italian sonnets can be divided into two parts, of eight lines and six lines. Here, because of the **rhyme scheme** (which does not follow the usual pattern), the two parts are more united, but can you still see a difference between them?
- The words of Ozymandias are in the form of a **command**, reflecting his status, but now they are **ambiguous**. When he was alive the 'mighty' would have despaired because they feared his power. Now they might despair because they too will end up like him.
- The broken statue is a **symbol** of the pointlessness of power and of mortality.
- The sands that 'stretch far away' can **symbolise** the passing of time, the loneliness of man or the emptiness of life.

My Last Duchess Robert Browning

The Poet

Robert Browning (1812–1889) was married to fellow poet Elizabeth Barrett. As well known for the romantic story of their elopement as for their poetry, they lived in Italy until her death in 1861, after which Browning returned to England, becoming very successful and internationally famous.

Content

The Duke of Ferrara is showing off his palace to an envoy (representative) of a Count, whose daughter the Duke wants to marry. He describes a picture of his 'last Duchess'. He says that she was too free and easy with her affections, so he gave orders to have her 'smiles stopped.' We can presume that he had her killed.

Character and Voice

The poem is written in the first person. Browning adopts a persona, so the voice is the voice of the Duke. The poem could be called a dramatic monologue, as it is almost like a play with only one character speaking. The Duke's character and motivation can be inferred from what he says. He does not realise how much he is giving away about himself.

The Duke is based on Alonso II, who ruled Ferrara, Italy, from 1559 to 1597, during the period known as the Renaissance, when it was common for noblemen to employ artists. His first wife, Lucrezia, died in suspicious circumstances. A few years later he remarried. Browning used the facts he knew to create a story of power, jealousy and murder.

Ideas, Themes and Issues

- **Jealousy and power**: the possessive Duke saw his wife with other men and became jealous, although there was no evidence she did anything wrong. He is a powerful man who wants to control everyone. He is happier with a painting of his wife than with the woman herself.
- **Love and death**: the Duke had a kind of twisted love for his wife. Love and death are intertwined.
- **Art**: the difference between art and life, or appearance and reality.
- **The human mind**: what turns a man into a murderer?
- **History**: the poet explores history by imagining the lives of historical figures. The Renaissance was a golden age of beauty and riches, but beneath that there was corruption and death.

Form, Structure and Language

- We are aware of the presence of a listener through **questions** and the use of the **second person**.
- The poem is written in **iambic pentameters**. The regularity of the metre and of the **rhyme (rhyming couplets** throughout) reflects the Duke's calmness and control in speaking of violent acts.
- The **diction** is informal. He quotes other people and the lines are broken up by **dashes** and other **punctuation marks**. This makes him sound casual and almost friendly.
- The painting, covered by a curtain that only the Duke can draw, is **symbolic** of his desire to control his wife.
- The statue of Neptune represents a powerful male figure taming a wild creature. This might indicate that the next Duchess will be treated in a similar way.

The River God Stevie Smith

The Poet

Stevie Smith (1902–1971) was brought up by her aunt, whom she called 'the lion aunt', in the suburbs of north London. She never married, looking after her aunt until she died in 1966. She worked as a secretary for a publisher, as well as writing poetry and novels.

Content

The river describes himself. He says he likes people to swim in him but if they are foolish and disobey the rules, he will drown them. He tells the story of a woman who has drowned and now lies on the river bed. He wants her to stay there. If she goes he will not forgive her.

Character and Voice

The voice here is not that of a person or even an animal, but of the river. The title turns a river in Hertfordshire into a god, recalling ancient pagan beliefs that everything in nature is inhabited by divine spirits. This is not a god that lives in the river, however, but the river itself.

The voice seems to be a male voice. He is aware of what people might think of him and at first seems modest and even playful. Later, however, he changes and shows that he is powerful and dangerous.

Ideas, Themes and Issues

- **The power of nature**: nature seems to have its own will. It is powerful and should inspire awe and fear in humans, who are powerless in comparison.
- **Men and women**: the river seems to be a male spirit. His attitude to the drowned lady might be seen as representing the attitudes of men towards women.

- **Love**: this is a strange sort of love. He will not let her go. He is possessive of the lady.
- **Death**: the river might represent death. He is frightening and takes people by surprise, yet he is seductive. Resting in his deep bed could seem attractive. However, he will not let anyone go. Now that she is dead, nobody remembers the lady.

Form, Structure and Language

- The poem is in the **first person**, with the poet adopting the **persona** of the river. **Personifying** the river as a god recalls ancient myths and makes the river more powerful and awe-inspiring.
- The poem is in one long **stanza**, letting one idea flow into another. At the start, the river talks about himself, before telling the story of the drowned woman. As it progresses, the poem becomes more serious and eerie.
- At first the river seems amusing and playful. The use of **rhyming couplets** and **half rhymes**, such as swimming / women and drowning / clowning, and the **colloquial** and jokey language he uses give the poem a **comic tone**.
- The poem seems to slow down towards the end. Lines 22 and 23 both start with a single word ('go' and 'now') which is carried over from the previous line. Then there is a **full stop**, making us pause and interrupting the flow of the poem.
- The last four lines are not in rhyming couplets. The effect of this is to **change the mood** and make us think about the serious subject of the poem.
- The last line is mysterious, leaving us with **questions** rather than answers. The lady is dead, so where would she want to go? How would she go? What does he mean by not forgiving her?

The Hunchback in the Park Dylan Thomas

The Poet

Dylan Thomas (1914–1953) was perhaps the most successful Welsh poet of the 20th Century. As well as his poems, which he often read on the radio, he wrote the influential play *Under Milk Wood* about life in a small South Wales town.

Content

The poet describes a tramp who spends his days in the local park. He eats bread from a newspaper and drinks water from the public fountain. The local boys make fun of him. After dark, when the park is closed, he sleeps in a dog's kennel.

Character and Voice

The voice is that of the poet, looking back at a character he used to see when he was a child. A hunchback is a person whose back, perhaps because of disease or deformity, appears to have a hump. The word is not as widely used now and most people probably know it from the story of the *Hunchback of Notre Dame*. Like the character in that story, Thomas's hunchback is a lonely figure, an outsider who is mocked or ignored by others.

Ideas, Themes and Issues

- **Childhood**: the poet shows us two sides of childhood – idyllic pictures of children playing in the park, free and innocent; and the cruelty of the boys towards the hunchback.
- **The outsider**: the hunchback is outside normal society. While the busy life of the park goes on around him, he is described as 'solitary' and remains alone through the day and night.

- **How we see others**: the hunchback is associated with dogs, showing that he is less than human in other people's eyes. In contrast, he creates an image of a woman in lines 32–34.
- **Imagination and escape**: the park is a magical place. Children create new worlds in their games and the old man creates a beautiful woman in his imagination. In spite of the boys, the park might be a refuge for the hunchback. At the end of the poem the park follows him to his kennel, suggesting that he is perhaps not as lonely or unhappy as others imagine.

Form, Structure and Language

- While the poet is in the poem and writes in the **first person**, he is there as an **observer**. He writes in the **past tense** about a childhood memory.
- There are seven **stanzas**, of equal length, each consisting of six lines. This **regularity** adds to the sense of routine – something that happens every day.
- There is very little **punctuation** and Thomas uses **enjambment**, letting not only the lines, but also the stanzas run into each other. At times this can be confusing, but it gives a sense of both the haziness of memory and the way time passes in the park. Also, there is no clear distinction between reality and imagination.
- The poet uses **rhymes**, but does not have a strict rhyme scheme. More often, he uses **half rhymes**, which are softer and help to convey a **melancholy atmosphere**.
- Natural **imagery** helps to make the park a place of escape, which is slightly unreal and magical. Trees, grass and the lake are **personified** as they, with the boys, 'follow' him out of the park.

The Ruined Maid Thomas Hardy

The Poet

Thomas Hardy (1840–1928) was a novelist as well as a poet. He was born and died in Dorset in South West England, and most of his work is set in this area, which he called 'Wessex'.

Content

A young woman on a visit to town meets an old friend who seems to be doing well, although when she lived in the country she was very poor.

Character and Voice

There are two voices. The first woman, who still works on the farm, is surprised to see how the other has turned out. She recalls what 'Melia' used to be like and wonders at how she has changed. Amelia's answer to everything is that it is because she is ruined. She has probably become either the mistress of a rich man or a prostitute.

These characters are typical of the rural people that Hardy wrote about, although here they are presented in a much more light-hearted manner than in most of his work. By being ruined, Amelia means that she has had sex before marriage. Because of this she would not be able to find a good husband and she would be something of an outcast. Yet her moral 'ruin' has led to her being apparently far better off than she was when she was virtuous.

Ideas, Themes and Issues

- **Rural poverty**: Amelia's comparative wealth and happiness contrasts with her former life, when she was 'dressed in tatters, without shoes or socks'. Many people worked very hard for low wages and had little prospect of escaping a life of poverty.
- **Women's lives**: Hardy shows us through his characters how few opportunities there were for women. Men would have had more freedom and would not have been judged as harshly.
- **Sexual morality**: Amelia is an outcast from her old life. Although people might think of her as a sinner, she does not seem to feel at all guilty. She is happy with her new life, while the 'good' girl is condemned to poverty.

Form, Structure and Language

- This poem has many features of a **ballad**, a poem or song that tells a story and is passed on orally. Hardy often used traditional forms like this, reflecting the fact that he is writing about 'ordinary lives'.

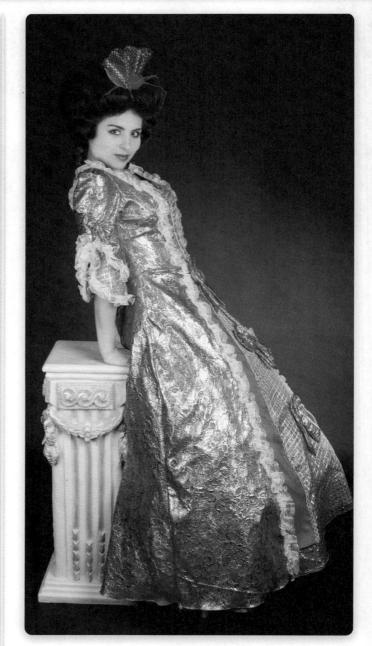

- It is in the form of a **conversation**, with speech marks indicating who is speaking.
- It has five **stanzas** of four lines each, with a simple regular rhyme scheme of **rhyming couplets**.
- It also has a strong simple **rhythm**, with four stressed syllables in each line, giving it an upbeat, song-like quality.
- There is a **refrain** at the end of each stanza, emphasising that the girl is defined by being 'ruined' and getting **humour** out of the **irony** of her situation.
- Hardy uses **dialect** to root the poem in the Wessex countryside.
- The **tone is ironic, light and humorous**, making us think about the subject in a different way.

Casehistory: Alison (head injury)
U. A. Fanthorpe

The Poet

For many years, Ursula Askham Fanthorpe (1929–2009) taught English at the girls' public school, Cheltenham Ladies' College. After giving up teaching she worked as a secretary, a receptionist and as a hospital clerk. Several of her poems, including this one, were inspired by the cases she came across at the hospital.

Content

A woman looks at a photograph of herself when she was young. She describes the girl as if she were a stranger. Alison has lost her memory. Every morning she has to be reminded of who she is.

Character and Voice

The poet takes on the persona of Alison, a woman who has suffered a head injury. She does not really remember anything of her childhood or youth, and has to be reminded every day. She is proud of her younger self and her achievements, but she knows something that her younger self does not know – what will happen to her.

Ideas, Themes and Issues

- **Youth and age**: she looks back on a time of innocence. The girl in the photo seems happy and secure. Although her father has died, she has 'digested' it and carried on with the confidence and certainty of youth. Now that she is older, Alison is a completely different person.
- **Memory**: we define ourselves by our memories. Alison has lost her memory and her sense of who she is.
- **Ordinary lives**: extraordinary things happen to ordinary people. There is nothing unusual or disturbing in the girl's background.
- **Mental illness / Unusual states of mind**: the poet tries to 'get inside' Alison's head. We can imagine and try to understand what it is like to be in her situation.
- **Lack of control**: we cannot predict or control what happens to us in life.

Form, Structure and Language

- The poem could be described as a **dramatic monologue**. The poet writes in the **first person** and the **present tense**, adopting the persona of Alison. The poem starts as if it is a speech in a play, with a 'stage direction' in brackets.
- There are nine short **stanzas**. Each has three lines, the first and third very short and the second quite long.

- The **regularity of the pattern** might reflect the repetitiveness of Alison's life. It also contributes to the rather **emotionless tone** of the poem. Alison could be talking about a stranger.
- The pattern of lines in each stanza suggests the way her mind is working, remembering things in short bursts.
- The first five stanzas focus on the photograph, **contrasting** her poise and delicateness with the harshness of Alison's condition: her leg 'lugs' her and her face is 'broken'.
- The next four stanzas focus on Alison now, trying to make sense of things. The **tone is matter-of-fact**, without self-pity.
- The final single line **repeats** a line from the first stanza. In the light of what Alison has said, it now has great **pathos**, emphasising Alison's alienation from her old self.

On a Portrait of a Deaf Man John Betjeman

The Poet

John Betjeman (1908–1984) went to Oxford University but failed to get a degree, later working as a teacher and as a newspaper editor before becoming one of Britain's most popular poets. He was made Poet Laureate in 1972.

Content

This poem was written in 1940, not long after the death of the poet's father. However, the deaf man is never named, nor is his relationship to the poet mentioned.

The poet is looking at a picture. He describes how the man in the portrait looks, before telling us what he was like when alive. Now he is buried in Highgate Cemetery, London.

Character and Voice

The voice is that of the poet. He looks back on his childhood and his relationship with his father. The main character, however, is his father – the deaf man.

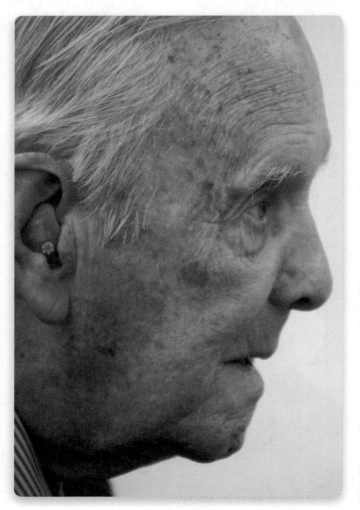

He is described as a rather old-fashioned man, who wore 'shooting clothes' and 'liked old City dining rooms'. He took his son on country walks and enjoyed painting landscapes. But he was deaf and could not hear birdsong or his son's voice.

Throughout the poem we are reminded that he is dead as the poet describes the physical reality of his death.

Ideas, Themes and Issues

- **Fathers and sons**: the poet remembers his father as a kind, wise man. It would seem to be a fairly happy relationship, but perhaps the father's deafness affected the relationship. It is used in the title to define him. Is there sadness in 'he could not hear me speak'?
- **Death and mortality**: the poet does not spare the details of death. Alongside pleasant memories of his father, he writes of the corpse in the cemetery. Memories do not make up for the fact that the man is dead. Nor can the poet see any hope of life after death.
- **Belief in God**: the poet speaks to God in the last stanza. However, it is only to say that he cannot believe in Him. He cannot believe in the soul, only in the decaying body.

Form, Structure and Language

- The poem is written in **ballad form**. Originally, ballads were folk songs or poems, passed on orally and not written down. They were usually dramatic stories taken from local history. Betjeman uses the ballad form to tell a personal story, about his father. Perhaps the form, like the fact that he does not say the man was his father, makes the story seem less emotional and his conclusions more rational.
- The poem consists of six **stanzas**, each of four lines. The second and third lines of each stanza **rhyme**. The first and third lines each have four stressed syllables and the second and fourth have three, following the traditional **ballad form** closely. This neat, regular pattern might seem surprisingly upbeat considering the subject matter.
- However, the last line is cut short. This might give a sense that the man's life has been cut short suddenly, that the poet has nothing left to say or that he is rejecting the easy pattern that belief in God can give to life.
- A lot of the poem's strength comes from the **juxtaposition** of pleasant **images** of the man in life with stark, morbid **images** of death.

Cluster 2: Place

Each of the fifteen poems in Cluster 2 focuses on a place, but each poet has his or her own way of responding to a place.

In the exam you will have to make connections between poems, looking at differences and similarities between the places described, and between the ways in which the poets present these places.

The places that inspired these poems are as varied as the poems themselves. They are set across the world in many different kinds of place.

Some of them identify the place in the title, for example, *London*, *Cold Knap Lake*, *The Wild Swans at Coole*. In others, the places that inspired the poems are not named, but they are clearly set in real places where the poets have lived and which have inspired them, for example, *Spellbound* and *The Prelude*. Often the poets are looking back on an important experience.

Most, but not all, of the poems are concerned with nature – its power as well as its beauty. There are lakes (*Cold Knap Lake, Crossing the Loch*), mountains (*The Prelude, Below the Green Corrie*), moors (*Spellbound*) and woods (*Wind, Storm in the Black Forest*). But there are also poems set in the urban landscapes of towns and cities (*A Vision, Hard Water, London*).

Sometimes the poet is alone in the landscape, reflecting on what it means to him or her; sometimes there are other people; and sometimes animals or birds.

When you read these poems, ask yourself:
- Why has the poet chosen to write about that place?
- What does the place mean to the poet?
- What impression does the reader get of the place?

As well as writing about what the places mean to them, the poets explore a variety of ideas, themes and issues. Here are some of the common themes in this cluster:

- **Memories** – *The Prelude, Cold Knap Lake, The Wild Swans at Coole, Hard Water, The Blackbird of Glanmore, Crossing the Loch, A Vision*.
- **Childhood** – *Cold Knap Lake, Hard Water, London, Price We Pay for the Sun*.
- **The people who live in a place** – *London, Price We Pay for the Sun, Cold Knap Lake, Neighbours, A Vision*.
- **Death and mortality** – *Neighbours, Cold Knap Lake, The Blackbird of Glanmore, London, Price we Pay for the Sun, The Wild Swans at Coole*.
- **The power of nature** – *The Prelude, Spellbound, Below the Green Corrie, Storm in the Black Forest, Wind, The Moment, Crossing the Loch*.
- **The beauty of nature** – *Crossing the Loch, Below the Green Corrie, The Wild Swans at Coole, The Prelude*.
- **Man and nature** – *Hard Water, Neighbours, Wind, Storm in the Black Forest, The Moment*.
- **Towns and cities** – *London, Hard Water, A Vision*.
- **Home / Belonging** – *Hard Water, The Blackbird of Glanmore, Spellbound, Wind, The Moment, Neighbours*.
- **The environment** – *Hard Water, A Vision, The Moment, Neighbours*.

Helpful Hint

Most of these poems are based on real places. If you live near any of the places described, it might be helpful to visit and see whether your response is similar to the poet's.

The Blackbird of Glanmore Seamus Heaney

The Poet

Seamus Heaney was born in County Derry, Northern Ireland in 1939. He grew up on a farm, the oldest of nine children.

Many of his poems are influenced by his childhood and he often writes about the beauty and cruelty of nature, and about the past. He was awarded the Nobel Prize for Literature in 1995.

Content

The poet notices a blackbird on the lawn when he arrives in Glanmore.

When he leaves it is in the ivy. The bird reminds him of when he was a boy and how, after his brother was killed in an accident, a neighbour talked about a bird on the shed roof. As he locks the car and the bird panics, he seems to see himself from the bird's point of view, 'a shadow on the gravel'.

Place

Glanmore is in County Wicklow, on the east coast of Ireland. Heaney moved there with his family in 1972, after resigning from his job at Queen's University, Belfast.

The place is not described in detail, apart from the gravel path, the grass and the ivy, but it is 'my house of life'. The focus is on the blackbird and the memories it evokes. It reminds him of another place – his childhood home.

Ideas, Themes and Issues

- **Memories:** the sight of the blackbird evokes memories of the poet's childhood. He remembers his younger brother. Here he does not go into detail about the boy's death. The memory is still with him but does not seem to disturb him too much.
- **Home:** Glanmore is the poet's home. The blackbird welcomes him and sees him off. Yet he also thinks of 'the house of death'.
- **Death and mortality:** he looks back to the death of his brother and thinks of his own death. The blackbird represents death and, at the end of the poem, he seems ready for it.
- **Man and nature:** man seems insignificant when looked down on from the bird's point of view.

Form, Structure and Language

- Each **stanza** of five lines is followed by an isolated single line. These lines would make sense if attached to the preceding stanza, so why are they separate?
- The poem is written in the **first person** and is clearly very personal. The poet shares the thoughts and feelings that are inspired by the sight of the blackbird. The poet speaks to the blackbird.
- The blackbird **symbolises** home, as he is on the grass to greet the poet, but he also becomes a symbol of death. He is 'in the ivy when I leave'. Ivy is often associated with death. Heaney remembers a neighbour pointing out a similar bird sitting on the shed roof at the time of his brother's death.
- The **gentle, sad mood** of the poem is helped by the use of **half rhyme**, such as 'arrive / life', the **repetition** of 'stillness' and the use of **sibilance**.
- The memory of childhood is made more vivid by the speech of the neighbour: 'yon bird'.
- The gentle mood is suddenly interrupted by the **onomatopoeia** of 'clunk'. This sound scares the blackbird and makes the poet see himself from the bird's point of view.
- At the end he seems to be addressing the blackbird as a friend, a **symbol** of home but also of death.

A Vision Simon Armitage

The Poet

Simon Armitage was born in Huddersfield, Yorkshire. After studying in Portsmouth and Manchester he worked as, among other things, a probation officer and a DJ before becoming a writer. He still lives in Yorkshire.

Content

The poet speaks about a time when town planners used to draw up plans for the future of towns and cities.

Sketches, plans and models of clean, modern, futuristic towns would be put on display for the public to see before they were built. The poet tells us that he found such architects' plans thrown away in a landfill site. The planners' dreams of the future never came true.

Place

The place described is a fantasy, but it is the sort of fantasy that many politicians, planners and architects have given to people, thinking it could become reality. In the 1950s and '60s, many towns and cities had large-scale plans for redevelopment.

On paper they looked attractive, promising a new, improved way of life. Some were built, some partially built and some never built at all.

Often those that were built proved disappointing: in recent years quite a few have been pulled down.

Ideas, Themes and Issues

- **Hopes and dreams:** the plans were not just for buildings but also for a new life. But the planners' vision was unrealistic and could never become reality.
- **Government and people:** the planners are seen as being out of touch with the people. The people in their plans are toys and their life nothing like real urban life.
- **The environment:** some of the plans concern the environment. There are bottle banks, electric cars and cycle paths. However, these improvements have not come about and, ironically, the plans end up in the environmentally harmful landfill site.
- **Time:** the future quickly becomes the past. There is a sense of regret – almost nostalgia – for a time when people were ambitious and hopeful.

Form, Structure and Language

- The poem starts with a **paradox**. The future is described in the **past tense**.
- After the first line the poet speaks directly to the reader, using an **imperative**, 'remember'. He is confident we will have similar memories to his.
- He uses the **specialised diction** of architects and planners.
- However, this impressive language is undermined by his use of **images** connected with toys and games. This makes it seem as if the planners were playing games, not seriously planning for the future.
- The first part of the poem describes the architects' plans in a way that makes them seem quite exciting. In the second part the poet introduces people 'like us' and the **tone** becomes gently mocking.
- The last four lines describe the poet finding the plans and the **mood** becomes sad as he thinks about how quickly the future becomes the past and how hopes and dreams disappear.

Helpful Hint

In this section you may come across words used to describe form, structure and language which you have not seen before. If you are unsure of their meaning, look them up in the Glossary of Literary Terms on pages 85–86.

The Moment Margaret Atwood

The Poet

Canadian writer Margaret Atwood is best known as a novelist. Novels such as *The Handmaid's Tale* have been described as science fiction, but Atwood prefers to call them 'speculative fiction', meaning that they are about things that could happen. She has won many literary prizes, both for her novels and her poetry.

Content

The poem describes the moment when a person feels that he or she has settled down somewhere, has come home and owns a place. At that moment nature pulls away from the person and says that it is the other way round. We do not own nature; nature owns us.

Place

The place could be anywhere. The poem is about an idea, rather than a particular place. It could be anyone's home. Some editions of this poem include a sort of postscript in brackets at the end that reads, 'morning in the burned out house'. This suggests that the poem came out of personal experience.

Ideas, Themes and Issues

- **Home:** people like to feel that they belong somewhere. They like the sense of achievement that comes from working hard, saving up and buying a place to call home. The poem warns us that we never really own anything.
- **The power of nature:** nature can embrace us but it can also destroy us. We cannot control nature.
- **The environment:** we can live in harmony with nature, but we should not try to control it.
- **Time:** we are only on Earth for a short time. People come and go but nature goes on.

Form, Structure and Language

- The poet addresses the reader with the **second person** 'you'. She uses the word to mean anyone, indicating that she is talking about a common experience.
- The poem is arranged in three **stanzas** of equal length. The first is about a person's sense of achievement at owning something. The **tone** is sympathetic to the home owner. However, in the second stanza the **tone** changes as nature withdraws its support: it is threatening and eerie. In the third stanza nature speaks to us directly.
- The **list** in the first stanza builds up from a room to a whole country, connecting ordinary private lives with the actions of nations. Perhaps we are responsible for more than just our own homes.
- Aspects of nature are **personified**. It is as if nature can choose whether or not to help us.
- In the final stanza nature speaks directly to us. It gives both an explanation of what has happened and a warning.
- The **images** used in the final stanza describe human achievement. These actions seem small and a bit ridiculous now, in contrast to the first stanza.

Preparation Task

Many of the poems in this section use personification when writing about nature. Find examples of this technique in other poems.
- What aspects of nature does each poet personify (e.g. trees, animals, the sun)?
- What human characteristics do the poets give to these things?
- What does this say about their attitudes to nature?

Cold Knap Lake Gillian Clarke

The Poet

Born in Wales in 1937, Gillian Clarke lives with her husband on a small farm. She has two sons and a daughter; and many of her poems are about family relationships. Others draw on her experience of farming and her sense of cultural identity.

Content

The poet recalls an incident from her childhood. She and her mother see a child being pulled out of a lake, apparently dead. Her mother resuscitates the child and her father takes her home. The child is beaten. Now the poet wonders whether she really did witness the incident.

Place

Cold Knap Lake is an artificial lake in Glamorgan, South Wales. The place is not described when the poet is re-telling the story, but a powerful picture of it is given in the fourth stanza. However, it could be a description of any lake anywhere. What matters is the water and what it signifies.

The lake represents the past and memory. She describes the 'troubled surface' and how the mud seems to 'bloom' when the swans take off. It is shadowy, surrounded by willows, and we cannot see what really lies beneath the surface.

Ideas, Themes and Issues

- **Memory:** the poem is based on a memory of a distant event. At the end, the poet questions whether memories are reliable. Are there things hidden in the past that we cannot remember?

- **Family relationships:** the poet admires her mother, who is described as a 'heroine' and who does not hesitate to help a stranger's child. Her father also helps by taking the child home. In contrast, the poor child is beaten, but this could be because of her parents' relief at finding her alive.
- **Childhood:** the poet and the drowned child have contrasting experiences of childhood. The events are seen through a child's eyes – vivid, simple and almost like a fairytale.
- **Nature:** although the actual lake is in a park, it is still dangerous and mysterious.

Form, Structure and Language

- The poet tells a story from her childhood, using the **past tense**. In the final two stanzas she switches to **present tense** as she wonders what the story means. So we have both the child's and the adult's viewpoints.
- As well as the **first person singular** (I), she uses the **first person plural** (we), emphasising the bond between her and her mother.
- The **imagery** draws on paintings and fairytales ('dressed in water's long green silk'; 'a heroine, her read head bowed'), making the event seem more distant and perhaps a little unreal.
- The willows are **personified**, with 'dipped fingers'. The lake is itself a **metaphor** for the past.
- The **question** in line 20 draws us into the poem, making us question our own memories.
- **Diction** associated with death and tragedy is used for the first two stanzas, but then there is a **positive image**, the child being compared to a lamb bleating.
- The **rhyming couplet** at the end is the poem's only rhyme. This helps to emphasise the point made. It almost 'wraps up' the subject and gives us an answer.

Price We Pay for the Sun Grace Nichols

The Poet

Grace Nichols was born in Guyana in the West Indies in 1950. She worked as a teacher and journalist before settling in Britain in 1977. As well as poems she writes children's stories, which are often based on Guyanese folklore and legends.

Content

The poet reflects on life in the West Indies. The islands may seem beautiful to tourists but life can be very hard for the people who live there. She concludes that 'poverty is the price we pay for the sun.' Is it a price worth paying?

Place

The poem does not seem to be about a specific place. It could be about anywhere in the Caribbean.

The islands attract tourists mainly because of the constant sun, warm weather and beautiful beaches. However, there are other aspects to the landscape and climate, such as volcanoes and hurricanes.

Life for the people of the islands is hard and most of them are poor.

Ideas, Themes and Issues

- **Appearance and reality:** most people see the islands as a tourist destination, but never look below the surface to see what life is really like.
- **Man and nature:** nature is powerful and dangerous. While the people described are almost at one with their landscape, it is not an easy relationship. Nature is full of hidden dangers and pain.

- **Heritage and culture:** the people are seen as belonging in the islands. The poet and her family have been shaped by the place they come from.
- **Poverty:** we are not given any details of the family's life, but a series of images shows how miserable their lives are. The final stanza tells us that the cause of their misery is poverty.

Form, Structure and Language

- The speaker seems to be talking to someone, whom she addresses as 'girl', about the reality of life in the islands. Perhaps this is a tourist, someone whose family had migrated from the islands or even her daughter. Maybe the listener is the poet herself and the **persona** is an islander.
- The poem is written in **dialect**. The speaker leaves out **verbs**: 'these islands real'. This conveys the speech patterns of the West Indies and helps the people of the island and their culture come to life for the reader.
- The poem is arranged in three **stanzas**. In the first the poet speaks about the islands, as if explaining what they are like. In the second she focuses on the people. In the short third stanza, she comes to her bleak conclusion.
- **Images** are taken from nature – specifically from the landscape and weather of the Caribbean – and used to describe the family. This makes them seem part of the landscape and the landscape part of them.
- **Sounds** are used to create atmosphere. The **alliteration** of 'while the wind… whipping' reflects the whistling sound of the wind, while the **sibilance** of 'sifting sands' conveys the movement of the sand.

Neighbours Gillian Clarke

The Poet

See page 41.

Content

The poet starts by looking back to 1986 when spring was late and the weather unsettled. Then the effects of the nuclear leak from Chernobyl, in the Ukraine, were felt throughout Europe. She goes on to write about this spring, considering how environmental disasters and diseases strangely unite people from different countries.

Place

The poem, like many of Clarke's, starts at home in the Welsh countryside. It broadens out to include the whole of Europe. She describes the scene in Finland and in Poland in 1986. Later, she speaks of every town in Europe being twinned to Chernobyl. Chernobyl is the town in Ukraine, formerly part of the USSR, where an accident in a nuclear power station led to widespread damage both to people's health and to the environment.

Ideas, Themes and Issues

- **Nature and the environment:** the accident at Chernobyl did a lot of damage to the environment, which lasted for years. The poet wants to broaden the debate from this particular incident to the more general issue of how we treat the planet.
- **Interconnection:** the way in which the effects of Chernobyl were felt as far away as Britain shows that national boundaries mean nothing. The environment and health are global issues, in which everybody is involved wherever they live.
- **History and politics:** the disaster had its roots in political and economic change, especially the break-up of the Soviet Union.
- **Hope:** The poem ends on a note of hope, although there is no real sense that we can change things.

Form, Structure and Language

- The poet uses the **first person plural** (we). This helps to make the issues personal and include the reader. She may be referring to herself and her family initially but later the 'we' includes the whole of humanity.
- The poem is organised into seven **equal stanzas** of three lines. The first four are in the **past tense**, each one focusing on a different place to show the effects of Chernobyl throughout Europe. The next three stanzas focus on the present. The last, with its very short lines, gives some hope.
- Although most of the poem is in **Standard English**, the last stanza uses **Russian** and **Welsh**. The poet uses the similarity between the Russian 'glasnost', used in the 1980s to mean openness in government, to the Welsh 'golau glas', meaning blue light. This emphasises the connection between the countries and turns it from a negative one to a positive one, the blue light giving hope.
- Natural **imagery** is used throughout, with birds and lambs, **symbols** of freedom and innocence, used with children to show the victims of environmental disaster.
- In the seventh stanza the poet uses an **image** taken from the Bible. Noah sent out a raven and then a dove to see if the flood was over. The raven did not return but the dove returned with an olive branch.
- The poem has been described by its author as a **polemic**, which is an attack on a policy or opinion. Here, the attack is a general one on politicians and industrialists who damage the environment.

Crossing the Loch Kathleen Jamie

The Poet

Kathleen Jamie was born in Renfrewshire, Scotland, and studied philosophy at Edinburgh University. She has travelled widely, especially in the Himalayas, but feels pulled back to Scotland. Her poetry reflects this 'split personality', exploring her sense of identity as a woman and a Scot. Recently, however, she has come to see herself as a 'nature poet'.

Content

A group of people, after a night out at a pub, row home across the loch. Impressed and a little frightened by their surroundings, the friends grow quiet. The poet wonders what lies under the water. The loch seems to glow with light and transform them into 'saints'.

Place

Loch is the Scots word for a lake. The particular loch is not identified. The people in the boat may live near the loch or they could be on holiday. Their cottage lies on the other side of the loch from the pub.

Ideas, Themes and Issues

- **The power of nature:** the poet is 'scared' on the loch. The wind, the water and hills seem threatening, the humans powerless in the middle of the loch. However, nature is also beautiful and the feeling we are left with is one of awe and wonder.
- **The environment:** beneath the stillness of the loch there may be 'ticking nuclear hulls'. They could be waiting to destroy nature.
- **Memory:** the poet shares a memory. She is unsure about the details but she hopes her friends remember, like her, the transforming experience.

- **Fear:** the experience frightens her. We cannot be sure what causes her fear – a sense that the loch is dangerous, perhaps, worry about what might be under the water or something else.
- **Friendship / Relationships:** the experience is shared with others. We do not know who the other people are, or how many of them there are, but it seems important that this is a shared experience, uniting them as 'saints'.

Form, Structure and Language

- At the start of the poem the poet asks the reader or listener to 'remember how we…' She includes the reader in her experience; at the same time there is a sense that the poem is addressed to her friends.
- She asks **questions**, as if looking for confirmation of the experience.
- The poet **juxtaposes** the familiar (the pub, the cottage) and the mysterious (the loch), making the experience stranger and more significant.
- She **personifies** the loch; it 'mouthed "boat"'.
- She uses **onomatopoeia** to convey the sound of rowing across the loch.
- She moves from negative ('the cold shawl of the breeze'; 'hunched hills') to positive **imagery** and **diction** ('phosphorescence'; 'shine') as her feelings change.
- The final image has **religious connotations**. They are a 'small boat of saints'. In the Presbyterian tradition, from which Jamie comes, saints are the people who have been chosen by God. The experience on the loch is an **epiphany** for all of them but how exactly they are changed is not clear.

Hard Water Jean Sprackland

The Poet

Born in 1962 in Burton-upon-Trent, Jean Sprackland writes both poetry and short stories. She looks for the 'mystery' in ordinary things and domestic life. She often writes about water.

Content

The poet remembers how, on holiday in Wales, she found that the water was different from the water she was used to at home. It was 'soft' rather than 'hard'. Hard water contains calcium and magnesium, which comes from the rocks where it originates, and has a slightly metallic taste. Soft water contains less of these elements, tasting more pleasant and creating more of a lather. But the poet prefers hard water, which reminds her of other things she likes about her home town.

Place

Burton-upon-Trent is a town in East Staffordshire. For a long time its main industry was brewing. While Sprackland is clearly writing about her home, and the language places the poem in the Midlands, the ideas and sentiments in the poem could apply to any industrial town.

Ideas, Themes and Issues

- **Home / Belonging:** the holiday in Wales provides a contrast with life in the town. She 'loved coming home'. Although her description of her home might not make it appeal to an outsider, the tone is one of affection and loyalty. She is aware that her roots have 'marked' her as 'belonging, regardless.'
- **Identity and heritage:** the water is characteristic of the place she comes from, just like the accent. She is aware that the town's industry has harmed the environment, but she is also aware of people's honest hard work in those industries.
- **Nature and the environment:** the hardness of the water is natural, coming from the rocks of the area she comes from. However, the air and the rain have been polluted by chemicals and industrial waste.
- **Education / Ambition:** 'book-learning' might have taken her away from her home, but the poet is aware of its limits and likes the idea of being brought down to earth by those who might think that her ideas and perhaps her poetry are 'too bloody deep'.

Form, Structure and Language

- The poet writes in the **past tense**, using the **first person**. Beginning as an **anecdote**, the poem develops into a reflection on her roots.
- It is organised into three **stanzas**. The first, three-line stanza briefly tells us about her experience in Wales. The second stanza explains what she likes about the water at home. The third stanza moves on to discuss the rain and the effects of pollution.
- Although most of the poem is in **Standard English**, it includes some words and phrases which are common in the Midlands to illustrate her point about the straight talk of the area: 'hey up me duck'; 'don't get mardy'.
- The hard water is **symbolic** of urban working class life. It represents both the positive and negative aspects of the poet's home town.
- Both tap water and rainwater are **personified**: 'honest water'; 'It couldn't lie'; 'this rain had forgotten the sea.'

Practice Question

Answer the following Foundation Tier question in 45 minutes. Answer both parts (a) and (b).

Part (a) What feelings about a place are expressed in *Hard Water*?

Part (b) Compare the ways the writers express their feelings about places in this poem and one other poem from 'Place'.

London William Blake

The Poet

William Blake (1757–1827) lived most of his life in London. He is known as both a poet and an artist, although in his lifetime he struggled to make a living and published his own work. He claimed to see visions and is sometimes called a 'mystic' or 'visionary'.

Content

The poet takes us on a journey with him through the streets of London and shows us some of the people who live there among the churches and palaces: children, chimney sweepers, soldiers and prostitutes.

Place

This is the London that Blake knew. It is the beginning of the Industrial Revolution and the city's ever-increasing population mostly consists of poor people, who struggle to survive. The buildings and the river represent authority and oppression. All the people in the poem seem to be victims.

Ideas, Themes and Issues

- **Authority and oppression:** Blake's sympathy is with the poor. The Church and State are represented by their buildings: the 'blackening church' and the 'palace walls'. Blake sees all authority as crushing the human spirit.
- **Poverty:** he gives a shocking picture of what life is like for the poor.
- **Corruption, sin and death:** the lives of Londoners are blighted by poverty and disease, any virtue or hope gone. The 'youthful harlot' is a figure of sympathy, but she is also responsible for the spread of disease.

- **Innocence and experience:** the poem is taken from Blake's *Songs of Experience*. On the surface it is possible to see innocence as positive and experience as negative, but innocence can also be seen as a state of childish naivety. There is more vigour and strength in experience, as well as a more realistic view of the world.
- **Revolution:** Blake was influenced by the ideas of the French Revolution. Poems like *London* can be seen as a warning of what might happen in Britain if things do not change.

Form, Structure and Language

- The poem is written in the **first person**. It is not about the poet, but it still seems very personal as he invites us along with him on his midnight walk.
- It is divided into four **stanzas** of equal length. Each stanza consists of one sentence in which he describes a new aspect of London life.
- Each stanza has four lines with a strong regular beat of four stresses per line and a regular **rhyme** scheme (*abab*). There is something relentless and inflexible about this, reflecting the seeming hopelessness of the subject.
- There is also a lot of **repetition** ('In every' and 'I hear') adding to the sense of the misery going on and on.
- The buildings – church and palace – represent the twin bodies of authority.
- The **diction** is negative and quite violent, giving the poem a **bleak and angry tone**.
- The **metaphor** 'mind-forged manacles' is **ambiguous**. Did people in authority forge the manacles to keep others in their place, or are we all responsible for our own 'manacles'?

From The Prelude William Wordsworth

The Poet

William Wordsworth (1770–1850) was one of the Romantic poets, poets who wrote mainly about nature and emotions. He lived most of his life in the English Lake District and was inspired by its beauty and grandeur.

Content

As a boy, on a summer's evening, the poet finds a boat and rows out into the lake. He aims for the top of a ridge that he can see on the horizon. As he rows on, another, higher peak seems to rise up behind the first. As he gets closer it cuts off his view of the stars. Frightened, he turns back. For a long time afterwards he is disturbed by the memory of that sight and what it might mean.

Place

The setting is a lake. The boy takes a boat from a 'rocky cave' on the shores of the lake. Although he does not name the lake, the 'craggy ridge' or the 'huge peak', they have been identified as Ullswater and its surroundings, a few miles from Hawkshead, where Wordsworth went to school.

Ideas, Themes and Issues

- **Nature:** nature is seen as a powerful force. When he was young, Wordsworth had an almost religious belief that nature was inhabited and powered by spirits. The awe and wonder he feels in the presence of nature is a sort of religious experience.
- **Growing up:** this episode represents an important step in his journey to adulthood, as he starts to think more deeply about the world and his place in it.

- **Poetry:** *The Prelude* is subtitled *Growth of A Poet's Mind*. Wordsworth has chosen this incident to show what made him into a poet. Creativity and the imagination are seen as spiritual things.

Form, Structure and Language

- This is part of a much longer poem, which tells the story of the poet's early life. This extract is from the first of thirteen 'books', which is entitled *Childhood and School-time*. This passage is a turning point in the story of the poet's childhood.
- The whole poem is a poetic **autobiography**. Consequently, it is written in the **first person** and in the **past tense**.
- The passage centres on a memory that he sees as having shaped his future – an **epiphany**.
- It has a steady but rather **gentle rhythm**. The use of **iambic pentameter** conveys the progress of the boat through the water and the beat of the oars. The **regularity of the metre** also controls and organises the very emotional experience of the boy as the adult poet reflects on it.
- Nature is **personified**, reflecting the sense that it has a life and spirit of its own. Nature itself is referred to as 'she' and guides the boy to the lake. The ridge is also feminine, 'an elfin pinnacle'. The huge peak, on the other hand, represents the darker side of nature. Powerful and threatening, it seems to chase the boy back across the lake.
- A change in **tone** is reflected in the language. As the peak appears, gentle, **positive diction** ('glitteringly'; 'sparkled'; 'lustily') is replaced by the language of violence and fear ('black'; 'upreared'; 'towered').

The Wild Swans at Coole W. B. Yeats

The Poet

William Butler Yeats (1865–1939) was born in Dublin but spent most of his childhood in London.

The family returned to Ireland when he was 16 and he went on to become one of Ireland's most celebrated poets.

He was part of a group of writers and artists who were interested in rediscovering Ireland's heritage and history, and in expressing its spirit through their art. He won the Nobel Prize for Literature in 1923.

Content

The poet describes a lake in autumn, where he has counted 59 swans. He recalls that it is 19 years since he first went there and tried to count the swans. Before he had finished, they flew away, but the experience cheered him up.

He says that everything has changed since then. Unlike him, the swans have not grown weary or sad. He reflects that one day he will find that they have gone – he wonders where.

Place

The lake described is in Coole Park near Gort in County Galway, Ireland. Coole Park was the estate of Yeats's friend, Lady Gregory.

He first visited Coole in 1897 in a state of physical and mental exhaustion. He once said that Coole Park was the most beautiful place in the world and during the following years he wrote many poems there. Coole Park is now a nature reserve.

Ideas, Themes and Issues

- **Nature:** nature is seen here as beautiful, mysterious and gentle. In the past it has helped the poet to heal.
- **Memory:** the lake and the swans remind him of his past. They make him think about how things have changed.
- **Time:** it is autumn and the poet is aware of the passing of time. He is conscious of how much older he is since he first saw the swans and how many things have changed. In contrast, the swans do not seem to grow old. At the end he thinks of the future.
- **Love:** he has been hurt by love and seems to be tired of it. He sees the swans as being untouched by sadness and still able to love: 'passion or conquest… attend upon them still.'

Form, Structure and Language

- The poet writes in the **first person**, revealing the feelings that the swans inspire in him.
- There are five **stanzas**. In the first, he describes the scene. The next two recall the past. The last two reflect on the swans and ask what will happen in the future.
- Each stanza has six lines and there is a **regular rhyme scheme**. Each stanza consists of a **quatrain** and a **rhyming couplet**. This regularity helps to make the poem seem calm and rather subdued.
- The **metre** also contributes to this effect. The poem is written mostly in **iambs** (the stress on every second syllable), where the beat is said to be like a heart beat, but Yeats varies this occasionally. The length of the lines also varies – the short lines give the sense of someone stopping to think.
- The season (autumn) and the **imagery** he uses to describe it reflect the poet's **mood** and his feeling that he is growing old.
- The swans are **symbolic** but could represent many things: love, happiness, even life itself.

Spellbound Emily Brontë

The Poet

Emily Brontë (1818–1848) is best known for her novel *Wuthering Heights*. She grew up in Haworth, Yorkshire, where her father was the minister. With her brother, Branwell, and her two sisters, Charlotte and Anne, she spent much of her childhood writing and inventing fantasy worlds. All three sisters became famous when their novels were published. After their early deaths the story of their lives became well known and 'the Brontë sisters' acquired almost mythical status.

Content

As the night draws in, a storm gathers in a bleak and lonely place. The poet is transfixed, unable to leave.

Place

The place is not mentioned by name and Brontë does not refer to any particular features of the landscape. However, we know that she only ever left Haworth for very short periods and was always unhappy when away. The 'wastes below' and the stormy weather identify the place as being the moors above Haworth.

Ideas, Themes and Issues

- **The power of nature:** the poet is surrounded by the storm. Its power is frightening, but fascinating.
- **Belonging:** this place is where she feels at home. She feels at one with the place and with the storm. She 'will not, cannot go'.
- **Loneliness and isolation:** the loneliness of the place might reflect her own sense of isolation and difference.

Form, Structure and Language

- The poem is written in the **first person** and in the **present tense**. This gives us the sense that we are sharing the poet's thoughts and feelings.
- The strong **rhythm** reflects the power of the storm. In the first two stanzas the **metre** is identical, with three stresses in each line, the first and second having an extra syllable at the end.
- In the third stanza, however, the first syllables of the first two lines are stressed ('clouds' and 'wastes'). What effect does this have?
- The unstressed extra syllable at the end of four lines is 'me'. Perhaps this reflects the poet's weakness and insignificance compared to the storm.
- **Repetition** is used throughout, including a **refrain** – the last line of the stanza, which is repeated with variations. Here it shows how, despite the weather worsening, the poet becomes more determined to stay.
- **Alliteration** ('bare boughs'; 'wild winds') combines with **repetition** to convey the relentless force of the storm.
- At the centre of this poem is a **paradox**. The night is unpleasant and it is dangerous on the moors, but the poet needs to be there.
- Brontë could be said to be using **pathetic fallacy**. The storm is a **metaphor** for her state of mind, which is not directly explained to us.

Preparation Task

There are two other poems about storms in this section: *Wind* and *Storm in the Black Forest*. Look at the words the three poets use to describe the storms. Are there any similarities? Which poet do you think is most successful in describing the power of the storm?

Below the Green Corrie Norman MacCaig

The Poet

Norman MacCaig (1910–1996) was born in Edinburgh. He attended the University of Edinburgh and for most of his working life was a primary school teacher. He divided his time between Edinburgh and the Highlands of Scotland.

Content

The poet describes a walk in the mountains during bad weather. The mountains seem threatening and dangerous in the dark, but he feels changed for the better by the experience. He climbs down and, as he turns to look back, the highest mountain is bathed in light.

Place

A 'corrie' (taken from the Gaelic word 'coire') is a round hollow on a hillside, sometimes containing a lake. The poem is set in the Scottish Highlands, probably near Lochinver, where the poet lived. Although the area is remote, it is popular with tourists, especially walkers and climbers, and is known for its dramatic scenery and changeable weather.

Ideas, Themes and Issues

- **Man and nature:** the mountains present a challenge for the walker or climber. They are dangerous, especially in 'ugly' weather. The poet does not, like some climbers, see himself as 'conquering' the mountains, nor does he feel defeated by them. He respects their power.
- **Adventure and excitement:** he sees his experience as exciting and thrilling, using the diction of adventure stories: 'swashbuckling', etc.
- **Inspiration:** nature inspires the poet and enriches his life. He is in awe of the mountains and feels a spiritual presence there.

Form, Structure and Language

- Written in the **first person** and the **past tense**, the poem is an account of a personal experience that changed the writer – an **epiphany**.
- It is divided into three uneven **stanzas**. In the first, the mountains seem threatening. In the second, the poet reverses our expectations as the mountains 'give' to him. The third stanza describes the effect of the experience on the poet.
- While the first two stanzas are short with fairly long lines, the third is long with shorter, uneven lines. There is a sense of excitement and maybe even of the poet being slightly out of breath.
- The poem starts with a **simile**, comparing the mountains to bandits. This makes them seem threatening, but also exciting.
- This idea is continued through **metaphor** throughout the poem. The mountains are **personified** as villains in a boys' adventure story.
- The poet takes our expectations of such stories and reverses them, referring to the **clichéd phrases** said to have been used by highwaymen.
- In the first stanza MacCaig uses an **oxymoron**, reflecting the mixture of emotions he feels, and he continues to use the **imagery** of light throughout the poem. This imagery has **connotations** of knowledge, revelation and inspiration.

Practice Question

Answer this Higher Tier question in 45 minutes.
Q Compare how poets write about the spiritual aspect of nature in *Below the Green Corrie* and one other poem from 'Place'.

Storm in the Black Forest D. H. Lawrence

The Poet

David Herbert Lawrence (1885–1930) is better known as a novelist than a poet. He came from a mining family in Nottinghamshire and many of his novels, such as *Sons and Lovers* and *Women in Love* are set in that area. His work was very controversial in his lifetime and, as a result, he spent a lot of his adult life abroad.

Content

The poet describes a storm breaking over the Black Forest. He describes the lightning, the thunder and the lack of rain. The scene makes him think about electricity and how mankind claims to have tamed it for his own use.

Place

The Black Forest (Schwarzwald in German) is an area of mountains and forests in South West Germany. Its wild natural beauty has made it a popular tourist destination, especially for walkers and climbers. The forest itself is not described in the poem, as the poet is looking up at the sky. Lawrence could be describing a storm anywhere at any time. However, the myths and fairytales of the region may have influenced him.

Ideas, Themes and Issues

- **The power of nature:** the violence of the storm, at once impressive and frightening, is an image of the awe-inspiring beauty of the natural world.
- **Man and nature:** is mankind really in control of nature? Lawrence seems to feel that we are deluding ourselves if we think we are. The modern, industrialised world relies on electricity, but we can never really control it or anything else in nature.

Form, Structure and Language

- The poem is arranged in five **stanzas** of unequal length. The first two describe different stages of the storm. The third, which has only one line, is about the rain – perhaps it is so short because the rain does not come so there is nothing to describe. The fourth stanza and the very short fifth give us the poet's interpretation of what he sees.
- The lines too are unequal in length. Some of them are **end-stopped**, but at other times the poet uses **enjambment**. This reflects the nature of the storm, stopping and starting again.
- Lawrence's use of **assonance** vividly conveys the experience. The poem moves from the heavy 'o' sounds of 'bronzey soft sky' to the short sharp sounds of 'i' : 'liquid fire, bright white '. So, from the still heavy sky the lightning strikes and the atmosphere changes with the change in sound.
- He makes the storm seem alive by his use of **verbs** such as 'spills', 'flutters' and 'wriggles'. A fork of lightning is compared, in a **metaphor**, to a snake and the sky is **personified**: 'the heavens cackle with uncouth sounds'. This line makes nature seem divine yet threatening.
- The **diction** of slavery and oppression is used to convey man's attitude to nature: 'mastered / chained, subjugated'.
- The final, two-word line, ending with an **exclamation mark**, sums up the poet's attitude. There is a mixture of amusement and cynicism about human power and delight in the storm.

Wind Ted Hughes

The Poet

Ted Hughes (1930–1998) was born in Yorkshire and attended Cambridge University, becoming well known as a poet in the 1950s. His first wife was American poet Sylvia Plath, who committed suicide. He was appointed Poet Laureate in 1984. Many of his poems are about animals and nature.

Content

The poet describes a storm that has been raging all night around the house. It continues in the morning and throughout the day. He goes out briefly and returns to the house. In the house he sits and watches the fire while the storm continues outside.

Place

The poem does not say where the storm is taking place. It could be a storm anywhere, around any house. However, the poet has said that it describes a gale that lasted a few days while he was staying at his parents' house, which was on top of a high ridge over the Calder Valley in West Yorkshire.

Ideas, Themes and Issues

- **The power of nature**: the storm is irresistible. As it rages, everything in nature seems to have a life and will of its own. The house gives some refuge but even there the poet does not feel safe. Man is insignificant compared to nature.
- **Relationships**: some people have said that the whole poem is a metaphor for Hughes's marriage. This might seem a bit far-fetched, yet it is clear in the final stanza that the two people in the house are not communicating. The storm might reflect their stormy relationship.
- **Home**: the house could be seen as a safe haven from the storm. However, the poet does not seem very confident that it can protect him.

Form, Structure and Language

- The poet uses the **first person** to describe a personal experience. Towards the end of the poem he changes from 'I' to 'we' and we realise there are two people in the house, trapped by the storm.
- The six **stanzas** follow the progress of the storm over a night and the following day. The first tells us about what happened in the night and the next three describe the following day. In the fifth stanza the poem switches from the **past tense** to the **present tense**. When the poem ends, the storm continues.
- The poet uses **enjambment** to connect lines and stanzas, reflecting the relentless progress of the storm.
- Nature is **personified**. The winds are described as wild animals ('stampeding') or angry spirits, destroying anything that gets in their way. Woods and fields are also personified.
- Hughes uses **metaphors** and **similes** to describe the storm's effect on the rest of the natural world. The hills are a tent and a bird is bent like an iron bar.
- The **simile** used to describe the house in line 17 conveys its fragility by comparing it to a fine goblet. The **alliteration** of the harsh 'g' adds to the effect.
- He also uses **alliteration** of 'w' and 'b' to convey the sounds of the storm.
- By the end of the poem everything seems to have come alive as the windows of the house 'tremble' and the stones 'cry'.

Cluster 3: Conflict

The fifteen poems in Cluster 3 are about conflict. The conflicts concerned are all violent, but each poet looks at violence and conflict in a different way. In the exam you will have to make connections between poems, looking at differences and similarities in the subject matter, and in how the poets present their ideas about conflict.

The conflicts (usually wars) that inspired these poems are as varied as the poems themselves.

Some of them are about an incident in a real war or armed conflict, retold by someone involved in it. *Futility*, for example, is based on the poet's experience in the First World War. *Belfast Confetti* is about Northern Ireland and *The Yellow Palm* is set in Iraq. In all these poems we get the sense that the poets were there and witnessed the events.

Other poets have written about events in which they were not personally involved. Tennyson wrote *The Charge of the Light Brigade* after reading about the charge in a newspaper. Both *Bayonet Charge* and *Mametz Wood* were inspired by incidents in the First World War but were written a long time afterwards.

Other poems do not refer to particular conflicts. *Next to of course god america* is about attitudes to war in general, while *Hawk Roosting* focuses on a bird of prey and leaves it up to the reader to infer ideas about human conflicts. '*Come on, Come Back*' is set in an imaginary war in the future.

The mood of these poems varies greatly. You will find anger here as well as sadness. You will find revulsion at the violence of war, admiration for those who fight, sympathy for its victims and hope for the future.

As well as the idea of conflict itself, the poets explore a wide variety of ideas, themes and issues. Here are just some of the common themes touched on in this cluster:

- **Power**: *Flag, At the Border, 1979, The Charge of the Light Brigade, next to of course god america i, Hawk Roosting*.
- **Loss and death**: *Mametz Wood, Futility, Falling Leaves, 'Come on, Come Back', Hawk Roosting, The Charge of the Light Brigade*.
- **The horror of war**: *Mametz Wood, The Yellow Palm, Bayonet Charge, Belfast Confetti*.
- **The futility (pointlessness) of war**: *Futility, next to of course god america i, Flag, The Falling Leaves*.
- **Patriotism**: *The Right Word, The Charge of the Light Brigade, Bayonet Charge, next to of course god america i, At the Border, 1979*.

- **Relationships**: *Poppies, At the Border, 1979, Futility*.
- **Nature**: *Bayonet Charge, Falling Leaves, Hawk Roosting, 'Come on, Come Back'*.
- **Combatants**: *Mametz Wood, The Right Word, Falling Leaves, Futility, Bayonet Charge, The Charge of the Light Brigade, next to of course god america i, 'Come on, Come Back'*.
- **Civilians**: *The Yellow Palm, At the Border, 1979, The Right Word, Poppies, Belfast Confetti, Out of the Blue*.
- **Fear**: *The Right Word, Out of the Blue, Bayonet Charge, Belfast Confetti*.
- **Hope**: *The Yellow Palm, The Right Word, At the Border, 1979, Out of the Blue*.

Helpful Hint

Remember that responding to poetry is not just about 'translating' or 'decoding' a poem's meaning. It is about what the poem makes you think and how it makes you feel. How do you respond to these poems? How do they make you feel about war and conflict?

Flag John Agard

The Poet

John Agard was born in British Guiana (now Guyana) in the West Indies in 1949. He moved to Britain in 1977 and has written many poems about his struggle to find a sense of identity as a man of mixed race and about the culture and history of the West Indies.

Content

Someone asks a series of questions about flags. What are they? The poet gives an answer to each question. He answers literally, saying that a flag is just a piece of cloth, but then says what, as a flag, it represents.

Conflict

The poem is not about a particular war, but uses the symbol of a flag to express the poet's feelings about war and imperialism. The flags could be flags of any nation.

Ideas, Themes and Issues

- **Patriotism**: a flag symbolises a country. People, especially soldiers, salute the flag to show loyalty to their country. According to the poet, patriotism is harmful, causing violence and death.
- **Imperialism**: flags are planted to lay claim to land. A flag can show that one nation has conquered another. The flag becomes a symbol of oppression and suffering.
- **War and conscience**: the flag 'blinds' people's consciences, perhaps giving them an excuse not to think about the morality of what they are doing.

Form, Structure and Language

- The poem consists of a series of **questions and answers**. The questions could be **rhetorical**, but the use of the phrase 'my friend' in the final stanza suggests that the poem is a **dialogue** between two people.

- The first four **stanzas** are very similar in form. The first line of each stanza starts with the same two words and the second line of each is identical. In the final stanza the question changes.
- Each stanza has three lines with the first and second lines **rhyming**, sometimes with a **full rhyme** and at other times with a **half rhyme**. The final stanza changes the pattern and ends with a **rhyming couplet**, giving the sense that these lines sum up the previous four answers.
- We know from the title that the subject is a flag, but in the **repeated** line about a flag being only a piece of cloth, Agard diminishes and mocks the idea of the flag, taking away its power and **symbolism**.
- He makes us question the idea of the flag by **personifying** it, drawing attention to the absurdity of such an insignificant thing causing so much suffering.
- The first four stanzas have a strong **regular rhythm**, with four stressed syllables in the first and third lines and three in the second. With the **rhyme**, this makes the poem upbeat and rather childish, in contrast with the serious subject matter. It is easy to read aloud. The final stanza does not follow the pattern, making the reader slow down. It is more thoughtful and downbeat.

From Out of the Blue   Simon Armitage

The Poet

Simon Armitage was born in Huddersfield, Yorkshire. After studying in Portsmouth and Manchester he worked as, among other things, a probation officer and a DJ before becoming a writer. He still lives in Yorkshire.

Content

This passage is from a long poem, commissioned for television in 2006 by Channel 5.

An Englishman, who works in New York, is trapped in the World Trade Center following the terrorist attacks. He imagines someone has spotted him as he looks out of the window, trying to attract attention by waving his shirt. He can feel the heat of the fire behind him but he does not want to do what others have done and jump out of the window. As the passage goes on he begins to lose hope.

Conflict

On September 11 2001 the terrorist organisation Al-Qaeda made a series of attacks on targets in America, using hijacked planes. One of the targets was the World Trade Center in New York, known as the 'twin towers'. Two planes were flown into the towers, causing them to collapse and killing nearly 3,000 people. The attacks were seen on television by viewers all over the world.

Many articles, poems, books and films have tried to make sense of the attacks. Armitage's poem was written to mark the fifth anniversary of the attacks (often referred to as 9/11). He says *Out of the Blue* is 'commemorative or elegiac, not political'.

Ideas, Themes and Issues

- **Fear**: the main emotion here is fear. Behind the speaker is the fire but, unless somehow he is rescued, the only way out seems to be jumping out of the window, which is equally terrifying.
- **Hope**: at the beginning of this extract the man clings to hope. Someone might see his white shirt waving. Someone might think he is worth saving and can be saved. As the extract goes on, though, hope fades.
- **Life and death**: he is fighting for survival. He is still breathing but only just. Soon he will have to face death.
- **History / World events**: Armitage shows us one man caught up in a conflict. We see what is happening through his eyes, focusing on a victim who has no say in what is happening to him.

Form, Structure and Language

- The **short stanzas** and **short lines** reflect the panic and perhaps the way the man is gasping for breath.
- The poem is in the **first person**, making the experience of the attack personal. Just from this extract it is not clear who the 'you' is. Possibly he is imagining someone he loves watching on television.
- The use of the **present tense** helps to make the experience vivid and immediate, especially the **repeated** use of the **present participle**: 'burning', 'waving', 'saving', etc.
- Armitage uses a lot of **repetition** and **rhyme**, adding to the sense of urgency and desperation.

Mametz Wood Owen Sheers

The Poet

Owen Sheers was born in Fiji and brought up in South Wales. He has won prizes for his poetry since 1999 and is considered one of Britain's best young poets. He recently presented a poetry series on the BBC.

Content

The poet describes how farmers would find the remains of soldiers who had died in battle for years afterwards. Now twenty soldiers have been buried together.

Conflict

During the First Battle of the Somme, one of the worst battles of the First World War, the 38th (Welsh) Division was given the job of attacking Mametz Wood. On 7 July 1916 the men were driven back by German machine gun fire from the wood. They were ordered to attack again on 10 July and reached the wood. By 12 July the Germans and their machine guns had been cleared out of the woods but the Welsh Division lost about 4,000 men.

The poem was inspired by the recent discovery of a grave (not at Mametz Wood) containing the skeletons of twenty soldiers, their arms apparently linked.

Ideas, Themes and Issues

- **Death**: the men have been dead for a long time. They are now only skeletons, outlasted by their boots. In death they are unidentifiable.
- **The waste of war**: there is no mention of why they fought or how they felt about the war. All the war means now is a few bones that get in the farmers' way.
- **Time and memory**: life goes on as the farmers continue to work in the fields. Memories fade but the discovery of the bones reminds us of the battle and the men's death.

- **Friendship / Comradeship**: the sight of the skeletons apparently linking arms might recall their relationship when they were alive. In the First World War men often served with friends from home and died with them, devastating communities.

Form, Structure and Language

- The poem is very **impersonal**. The poet is not a part of the story and none of the soldiers are identified. Nor are the people who found them. This helps to give the poem a **melancholy tone**, as there is something sad about not knowing who the men were. But is it too impersonal, lacking sympathy perhaps?
- The third stanza refers directly to Mametz Wood. The men being told to walk rather than run makes them seem like schoolboys, showing their innocence and lack of choice. The machine guns are described as 'nesting' as if they are birds.
- The **images** used to describe the remains emphasise their fragility and the fragility of life itself: they also show how they are no longer individuals, no more human than a plate or a bird's egg.
- The earth is **personified** and, using **military language**, compared to a guard, standing sentinel over the soldiers' remains.

Practice Question

Answer this Foundation Tier question in 45 minutes. Answer both parts (a) and (b).

Part (a) What ideas about war are explored in *Mametz Wood*?

Part (b) Compare the ways in which ideas about war are presented in this poem and one other poem from 'Conflict'.

The Yellow Palm Robert Minhinnick

The Poet

Robert Minhinnick was born in Neath, South Wales in 1952. He is a poet, essayist and environmental campaigner. He was a co-founder of both Friends of the Earth (Cymru) and Sustainable Wales.

Content

The poet tells us about his walk down Palestine Street. First, he sees a funeral passing by. Then he hears the call to prayer and looks into the mosque. Then he meets two beggars and gives them money. He sees a Cruise missile, also watched by a beggar child. He sees the same child reach up to touch a palm tree and the dates from it fall into his arms.

Conflict

Minhinnick was inspired to write this poem when walking down Al-Rashid Street in Baghdad, Iraq, in 1998. In December 1998, British and American forces bombed the city. This was a few years after the war which followed Iraq's invasion of Kuwait and which Saddam Hussein, the Iraqi president, called 'the mother of all wars'. In 2003 British and American forces again invaded Iraq.

The city described here is a city scarred by war.

Ideas, Themes and Issues

- **Culture and tradition**: signs of Arab culture are all around. However, the traditional way of life is threatened. The funeral is for a man who has breathed poisoned gas. There is blood on the walls of the mosque.
- **Poverty**: the city is a city of beggars.
- **Victims**: all the people the poet mentions are victims. Their suffering could be the result of war or of oppression and poverty.

- **Hope**: until the final stanza there seems to be little hope. But, the last thing the poet sees is the yellow palm tree, which gives its fruit to the beggar child.

Form, Structure and Language

- The poet has described this poem as a **ballad**. Like a traditional ballad it has a very **strong rhythm**, with alternate lines having four and three stressed syllables.
- Like many ballads every second line **rhymes**.
- Unlike most ballads, there are six lines per stanza.
- Ballads usually tell a story. The **repeated** line 'As I made my way down Palestine Street' suggests that the poet is telling a story but it is only the story of what he sees as he walks down the street. It is more like a series of pictures, one to each stanza, each showing a different aspect of life in Baghdad.
- The poem is in the **first person** but the poet is an observer of the scene rather than a participant.
- The poet uses all his senses to make the city come alive. He 'watched the funeral', 'heard the call to prayer', pressed money into the beggars' hands, 'smelled the wide Tigris' and perhaps tasted the dates.
- **Images** of traditional life are **juxtaposed** with **images** of modern warfare: 'lilac stems' and 'poison gas'; 'caravan' and 'Cruise missile'.
- The yellow palm of the title could be **symbolic** of hope and peace. The dates are 'sweeter than salaams'. A salaam is a formal greeting, the word itself meaning 'peace'.

The Right Word Imtiaz Dharker

The Poet

Imtiaz Dharker was born in Pakistan and has lived in India and Britain. She works as a poet, artist and documentary film maker. Her poems explore childhood, religion, violence and culture.

Content

The poet sees a stranger outside in the shadows. She speculates on who it might be and wonders about the words used to describe someone who can be seen as a terrorist, a freedom fighter, a militant, a martyr, or a child.

Conflict

The poem does not describe a particular conflict, but focuses on the idea of terrorism. It could be taking place almost anywhere in the world in the present day.

Ideas, Themes and Issues

- **Perception**: the poem explores how, in a conflict, the same person can be seen in many different ways, depending upon whether you share his views and ideas. One person's terrorist is another person's martyr.
- **Language**: the poet explores how the words used to describe someone carry associations that betray the speaker's attitudes, and inspire feelings in the listener. She is searching for the 'right word', but language has its limits: 'no words can help me now'.
- **Fear and violence**: the poem reflects a world where people are afraid and suspicious, with the threat of violence ever-present.
- **Innocence**: towards the end of the poem the figure in the shadows is seen as a young boy. He should be innocent but his eyes are 'too hard'.
- **Hope and reconciliation**: there is hope at the end of the poem, arising from a feeling of empathy: the boy could be anyone's son. The poet reaches out to the boy and invites him into her house. He takes his shoes off in a respectful, almost religious, gesture. We do not know what happens next.

Form, Structure and Language

- The poem is written in the **first person** and is in the **present tense**. This gives us a sense that this could be happening to anyone now, adding to the tension of the situation. The poet seems to be talking directly to us, sharing her changing ideas.
- There are nine short **stanzas**. Each of the first seven contains a new definition of the person in the shadows.
- The lines, like the stanzas, are short, adding to a sense of urgency and reflecting the speed with which the poet is thinking, as she constantly changes her mind.
- The **repetition** of 'outside the door' and 'in the shadows' reinforces the sense of fear. The subtle changes from 'the door' to 'your door' and then to 'my door' suggest that she is writing about a common experience, rather than one particular event.
- The poet asks **questions**, as she searches for the best **description**, making readers think about what their feelings and reactions might be in this situation.
- The words she uses to describe the boy are all **emotive terms**, laden with assumptions from different political points of view. Finally she uses **simple words** that seem neutral: 'boy', 'son' and 'child'. However, these words too are emotive: they imply innocence.

At the Border, 1979 Choman Hardi

The Poet

Choman Hardi is a Kurdish poet who lived in Iran, Iraq and Turkey before coming to Britain in 1993. She originally wrote in Kurdish but now writes mainly in English. She says her poems are the poems of exile and her experience reflects that of many Kurds. This poem is about her family's move from Iraq to Iran in 1979.

Content

The poet remembers how, aged five, she moved with her family from one country to another. She expects everything to be different. Her mother says that they are going home and everything will be better. As their papers are checked, the girl compares the two sides of the border. They are the same.

Conflict

Kurdistan is a mountainous area of the Middle East, divided between Iraq, Iran and Turkey. As a minority ethnic group, the Kurds have been persecuted in all three countries, especially in Iraq under Saddam Hussein. There have been several attempts by Kurdish nationalists to gain greater independence for their regions or to establish an independent country of Kurdistan. In 1979 Kurds in Iran rebelled against the government and gained control of an area bordering Iraq. Hundreds were killed. The fighting continued until 1983 when the Iranian government regained control. However, violent conflicts have continued and many Kurds continue to go into exile.

Ideas, Themes and Issues

- **Home**: the family and the other people at the border feel that they are coming 'home'. It is important for people to believe that they belong somewhere.
- **Nations**: the border is where one country ends and another begins. The adults are convinced that life will be better in their 'new' country, but the child can see no difference. It is interesting that the countries are not named. There is something arbitrary about a border.
- **Childhood / Memories**: the poet remembers how she felt as a child. It is as if only a child can see clearly. She cannot see the difference between the countries.

Form, Structure and Language

- The poem describes the poet's personal experience, using the **first person**. She uses the **plural** 'we' to stress that it is also about her family and community.

- The story is told from a child's point of view. Although the poet is an adult remembering the experience, she does not reflect on it or comment on it.
- The language of the first four **stanzas** is simple and straightforward, including direct speech. It reflects the **simplicity** of the child's point of view and the way adults, like her mother, speak to her.
- The iron chain **symbolises** the division between the countries. The words 'border', 'check-in' and 'chain' are **repeated** throughout the poem, emphasising the man-made divisions.
- In the final line the word 'chain' is used again but this time to describe the mountains. Humans might create borders but the mountains, the soil and the rain do not recognise them.

Belfast Confetti Ciaran Carson

The Poet

Ciaran Carson was born in Belfast in 1948. Unusually, his family spoke Irish at home. He sees his bilingual upbringing as an important influence on his poetry. He studied English at Queen's University Belfast and spent several years travelling round Ireland playing folk music. He still lives in Belfast and teaches at Queen's University.

Content

The poem describes a riot in Belfast. The army's riot squad is attacked. A bomb goes off. The poet tries to escape but finds all the streets are blocked. He is in an area he knows well, but he cannot find his way out. At the end he is stopped by the army and questioned.

Conflict

The poem is set during 'the Troubles' in Northern Ireland. In the 1960s, tension between Catholic and Protestant communities erupted into violence, and paramilitary groups such as the IRA and UDA became involved. The British army was sent to keep the peace, but during the 1970s the violence escalated, continuing into the '90s. One of the most dangerous areas of Belfast was the Falls Road area, where Carson was brought up. He lived in Belfast throughout the period.

The poet has said that the term 'Belfast confetti' refers to bits of metal such as nuts and bolts, which men used as weapons when there was a riot in the Belfast ship-yards. Such objects were also used in homemade bombs.

Ideas, Themes and Issues

- **Violence**: the poet is not concerned with the politics of the situation. He concentrates on one violent incident, vividly portraying what it is like to be caught up in it.
- **Fear**: the overriding emotion is fear. He is desperate to escape the violence.
- **Home**: the incident happens near his home. The familiarity of the setting makes the eruption of violence more shocking.
- **Language**: language helps people to make sense of things. However, here, language is breaking down and he is unable to make sense of the situation.

Form, Structure and Language

- The poet uses the **first person** to share a personal experience with the reader.
- The first stanza is written in the **past tense**. This changes dramatically to the **present tense** in the second stanza. The experience is not over, but is happening now.
- The lines are long. However, they are broken up with **punctuation marks**.
- The **imagery** of punctuation – asterisks, hyphens, etc. – is used very precisely to describe each stage in the riot. The writer cannot finish a sentence in his head as he keeps coming across these punctuation marks.
- The names of the streets he mentions (all of them real streets, including the one where the poet was brought up) recall the Crimean Wars 100 years earlier.
- In the last two lines he uses the details of their equipment to describe the soldiers. This makes the experience **impersonal**, perhaps inhuman.
- The **questions** in the last line are asked by the soldiers who stop him, but he could be asking them of himself as he tries to make sense of what is going on.

Poppies Jane Weir

The Poet

Jane Weir lives in Derbyshire and is a designer as well as a poet. She was commissioned to write this poem by Carol Ann Duffy as part of a feature on war poetry in *The Guardian* in 2009.

Content

A woman pins a poppy on her son's blazer and sees him off. Presumably, he is in the armed forces and is going away to fight. When he has gone, she goes for a walk and finds herself in the graveyard, reading the war memorial.

Conflict

No particular war is mentioned here, although the poet has indicated that she is concerned with the mothers of soldiers serving in Iraq and Afghanistan. The reference to Armistice Sunday at the beginning of the poem connects it with other wars, particularly the First World War.

Ideas, Themes and Issues

- **Mothers and sons**: the poet's main focus is the feelings of the mother. She helps her son to get ready, fussing over his appearance, as she tries to be 'brave' about losing him.
- **Memories**: the woman remembers playing with her son when he was a small child and a reference is made to this at the end of the poem. We do not know what happens to the boy but we are aware that she could be left only with memories.
- **History and the individual**: the poem does not tell us where the woman's son is going. The experience is generalised; it could be any war at any time, emphasised by the references to the poppies. The poem reminds us that wars affect individuals' families and loved ones.

Form, Structure and Language

- The poem is written in the **first person**, the poet imagining how it would feel to be the mother of a son going away to war. She addresses the son directly, even though he is not there, using the **second person**.
- She writes in the **past tense** as she recounts an incident from the recent past. It is a story without an end, as she does not reveal where her son has gone or what has happened to him.

- Both the poppy, representing the sacrifice of lives in war, and the dove, representing peace, are common but powerful **symbols**. The song bird the mother releases from its cage could represent her 'letting go' of her son.
- The poet uses a lot of **imagery**. She uses **similes**, for example, the simile in lines 20–21 expresses the possibilities that lie outside the home for the boy; the reference to a wishbone expresses her hope and her fragility. She uses **metaphors** taken from sewing to express her feelings after he has gone (e.g. in line 28) and she compares the dove in the sky to an 'ornamental' stitch. Using imagery taken from domestic, usually female, tasks emphasises the traditional role of the mother.
- The **tone** is sad but hopeful. It is interesting that the poet never states explicitly that the boy is a soldier or is about to go to war. This is implied by the references to war graves and poppies. Apart from that it could be about any woman saying goodbye to any son. Does this make it a stronger or a weaker poem for you?

Futility Wilfred Owen

The Poet

Wilfred Owen (1893–1918) was born in Oswestry, Shropshire and brought up in an evangelical Anglican family. He was sent to France as an Army Officer in 1917. He suffered from shellshock after experiencing the horrors of trench warfare and was sent to Craiglockhart hospital in Edinburgh to recover. It was there that he started to write about the war. In 1918 he was sent back to France and was killed seven days before the war ended.

Content

The speaker tells someone to move a fallen soldier into the sun. He says that if anything can wake him, the sun can. It woke him at home, where he worked on a farm, and it has woken him every morning since he came to France. The poet questions why, if the sun can make seeds grow and made the Earth come alive, it can do nothing for the soldier.

Conflict

The First World War (1914–1918) was one of the bloodiest conflicts in history. Over 15 million people were killed, many of them in the trenches of Northern France and Belgium. Modern weaponry and poor leadership made the experience of war especially horrific. The work of writers such as Siegfried Sassoon, Rupert Brooke, Isaac Rosenberg and Wilfred Owen conveyed the horror and waste of war to people at home and to subsequent generations.

Ideas, Themes and Issues

- **Futility** means uselessness, pointlessness or having no effect. The poet could be thinking of the ineffectiveness of his hope that the sun will revive the soldier, the pointlessness of the soldier's death or the war, or even of life itself.
- **Hope and hopelessness**: the speaker hopes that his comrade might still be alive or that the sun might somehow revive him, but this does not happen and he is left without hope.
- **Death**: death is final. Nothing can bring back the dead, not even the life-giving sun.
- **Friendship / Comradeship**: the relationship between the poet and his fallen comrade brings home the reality of war. He sees him as an individual and his attitude to him brings humanity into an inhumane situation.

Form, Structure and Language

- The poem begins with an **imperative** or **command**, which could be an officer giving orders to his men.
- There are two **stanzas** of equal length. After the initial command, the first reflects on the soldier's life and seems to contain the hope that he is still alive or might come back to life. In the second stanza he asks why the sun is powerless and the soldier cannot be brought back to life.
- Owen uses **half rhyme** (sun / unsown; tall / toil) as well as **eye rhyme** (know / now). The effect of this is gentler and subtler than full rhyme.
- The poet uses a lot of **natural imagery**. The image of the 'fields unsown' tells us about the soldier's life before the war, working on a farm. Now his life has been cut short in the snow.
- The sun is **personified**. At first it is like a figure in a children's story: 'the kind old sun'. It is seen as powerful but in the end cannot help. It might also be a **symbol** of hope or even of God.
- The tone changes dramatically from the first to the second stanza. The first is gentle and flowing. The second is broken up with **dashes** and **question marks** as the poet looks for answers in vain.

The Charge of the Light Brigade
Alfred, Lord Tennyson

The Poet

Alfred Tennyson (1809–1892), was one of the most popular poets of the Victorian age. Born in Lincolnshire, he published poetry from an early age, but only became successful in the 1840s. In 1850 he became Poet Laureate and was greatly admired by Queen Victoria and her husband, Prince Albert.

Content

The men of the Light Brigade are ordered to charge into a valley. Although they may know that the order was a mistake, it is not for them to ask why. They obey orders.

In the valley they are surrounded by the enemy's cannons, but they ride bravely on. They break through the enemy lines, attacking the Russians with their sabres before retreating.

The few that are left ride back through the valley, still being shot at. The poet asks that their bravery be honoured.

Conflict

The Crimean War (1853–1856) was fought between the Russian Empire and an alliance which included Britain, France and Turkey.

The causes of the war were complex but most people in Britain felt that it was justified. The charge described in the poem took place during the Battle of Balaclava on 25 October 1854.

The British commander, Lord Raglan, ordered the brigade to attack the Russian forces in order to prevent them carrying off some guns they had captured. But the message was delivered wrongly and Lord Cardigan led a cavalry charge into the valley ahead, instead of to the left. Around half the brigade were killed, captured or injured.

Ideas, Themes and Issues

- **Patriotism**: the soldiers fight for their country. Tennyson does not question the idea of patriotism or of doing one's duty. The result is tragic but also glorious.
- **Bravery**: the men are undoubtedly brave. Their courage is emphasised throughout and we are encouraged to admire them.
- **Leaders and men**: although the men are 'noble', those who command them are implicitly criticised. Tennyson does not blame anyone in particular but 'someone had blundered'.

- **Death and remembrance**: it is important to remember the dead. Tennyson asks us to remember their bravery. Perhaps he also wants us to remember the 'blunder' that caused their death and to learn from it.

Form, Structure and Language

- The poem consists of six **stanzas** of varying lengths, each of the first five describing a stage in the action. The final stanza reflects on the action.
- The pattern of one stressed syllable followed by two unstressed is known as **dactylic**. This is quite unusual in English verse.
- This **strong rhythm** might remind the reader of the beat of the horses' hooves and the pounding of the shot. It gives a sense of speed and excitement. The fact that each line starts strongly with a stressed syllable and ends on an unstressed syllable might reflect the ultimate failure of the action.
- The **rhyme scheme** is irregular.
- Tennyson uses a lot of **repetition**, especially at the beginning of lines. This reflects the relentless attack of both the Light Brigade and the enemy cannons.
- Each stanza ends in a **refrain**, identical in the first three stanzas, but varied in the last three. This emphasises the size of the brigade, which was hugely outnumbered.
- In the final stanza Tennyson speaks directly to readers, urging us to honour the men of the Light Brigade.

Bayonet Charge Ted Hughes

The Poet

Ted Hughes (1930–1998) was born in Yorkshire and attended Cambridge University, becoming well known as a poet in the 1950s. His first wife was American poet Sylvia Plath, who committed suicide. He was appointed Poet Laureate in 1984. He is probably best known for his poems about nature, but he also wrote a lot about war.

Content

A soldier is described as he takes part in a bayonet charge. He runs across a field towards a green hedge through a hail of bullets. Confused, he almost stops. Then he sees a hare. He runs past it towards the hedge, all thoughts of patriotism and honour disappearing in his desperate run to escape the bullets.

Conflict

The war is the First World War, which ended nearly 40 years before Hughes wrote the poem. However, he kept returning to the theme, especially early in his career. His father had survived the Battle of Gallipoli, where most of his regiment was killed, and his experiences were a great influence on Hughes, as was the work of war poets such as Wilfred Owen (see page 62).

A bayonet is a blade attached to a rifle. When soldiers went 'over the top' out of the trenches, they would charge the enemy with their bayonets fixed ready to stab enemy soldiers rather than shoot them.

This poem is not about a particular battle and perhaps not just about the First World War. Hughes's concern was with war in general.

Ideas, Themes and Issues

- **The horror of war**: the poem vividly conveys the horror of being part of a bayonet charge. The young soldier is surrounded by bullets. Hughes does not describe the dead or dying, but the yellow hare might represent them. The overriding emotion is fear.
- **Patriotism**: the soldier has been given reasons to justify war. In the battle, ideas like patriotism and honour are meaningless.
- **The individual / Humanity**: Hughes focuses on one person. The soldier must be surrounded by others but they are not mentioned. In imagining how one person might feel, he makes us think about how any of us might feel in that situation. War is about real, individual people, not just nations and armies.

Form, Structure and Language

- The poem focuses on one man. Hughes isolates his experience by not mentioning any of his comrades.
- The lack of other people in the poem also conveys the inhumanity of war. The experience seems unreal, almost dream-like.
- The poem is written in the **past tense** and is divided into three **stanzas**. The first describes the soldier running towards the hedge. In the middle stanza, time seems to freeze. In the third, the action starts again.
- The **diction** emphasises the soldier's youth and inexperience: 'raw'; 'bewilderment'.
- Hughes uses **similes** to convey the physical and mental pain of the soldier in lines 6, 8 and 15.
- The yellow hare, appearing unexpectedly, provides a horrific **image**. Why does he choose to describe an animal running across the field rather than another man?

The Falling Leaves Margaret Postgate Cole

The Poet

Although she came from a privileged background, Margaret Postgate Cole (1893–1980) became a socialist and feminist early in her life. She was a pacifist during the First World War, campaigning against conscription. However, when the Second World War started, she gave up pacifism and supported the war.

Content

The poet reflects on a journey in the autumn. She sees leaves falling from the trees and is reminded of the many soldiers killed in the war.

Conflict

The poem was written in 1915 during the First World War. Millions of soldiers from both sides were killed, many of them in the trenches of Northern France and Belgium (Flanders). Many people at home, not just pacifists, were very critical of politicians and army commanders for their running of the war. Not long before this poem was written, over 50,000 British soldiers were killed in the Battle of Loos.

Ideas, Themes and Issues

- **Death and mortality**: the image of the leaves emphasises just how short and fragile human life is.
- **The waste of war**: a 'multitude' has perished. The sheer number of the dead is tragic. People often spoke about a 'lost generation' of men who died during the war. The tragedy is that they did not live long enough to die of old age or disease.
- **Mourning**: written from the point of view of a woman at home, the poem focuses on her reaction, rather than the reality of the battlefield. She is not writing about first-hand experience, but about something she and her readers have read or heard about.
- **Casualties** were so great that almost everyone would have known someone who was killed. This poem is not about a particular man's death. But it could be described as an elegy, a poem of mourning for the dead.

Form, Structure and Language

- The poem is written in the **first person** and the **past tense**, adding to the **mood of reflection**.
- The **natural imagery** (leaves and snowflakes) and the experience of riding on an autumn day – beautiful, gentle and peaceful – **contrast** with the reality of war.
- The poet's use of sound, such as **alliteration** and **onomatopoeia** in line 4, helps to create a melancholy and slightly eerie atmosphere.
- The falling leaves **symbolise** the fallen soldiers, both in their fragile beauty and their numbers.
- The **diction** used about the soldiers is positive: they are 'gallant' and (in spite of what the reality might be) beautiful in death. They are seen as victims, not aggressors or even willing participants in war.
- All of this creates an **elegiac mood**. An elegy was traditionally a poem mourning the death of a friend or a well-known person, but can also be a poem that reflects on death in general.

Practice Question

Answer this Higher Tier question within 45 minutes.

Q Discuss how the poets use imagery to convey ideas about conflict in *The Falling Leaves* and one other poem from 'Conflict'.

'Come On, Come Back' Stevie Smith

The Poet

Stevie Smith (1902–1971) was brought up by her aunt, who she referred to as 'the lion aunt', in the suburbs of north London. She never married, looking after her aunt until she died in 1966. She worked as a secretary for a publisher, as well as writing poetry and novels.

Content

The poem is subtitled 'incident in a future war'. After a battle has been fought at Austerlitz, a girl soldier is left barely alive and with no memory. She gets up and staggers over to a lake, takes off her uniform, plunges into the cold water and swims out into the lake. She drowns. An enemy guard finds her clothes and, while he waits for her to return, carves a pipe out of the reeds. On it he plays a popular song, 'Come On, Come Back'.

Conflict

Smith imagines a war in the future. The soldier is female and she seems to have been wounded by a chemical weapon. The poem also refers to the past. Austerlitz was the scene of one of the most important battles of the Napoleonic Wars in 1805. Memel is a town in Lithuania, which was handed over to the Germans during the Second World War and was besieged by the Soviet army in 1944.

Ideas, Themes and Issues

- **The inevitability of war**: Smith imagines a future war. Her references connect it to past wars. She does not see things changing except in the details.

- **Men and women / Women at war**: at the time when she wrote the poem (the 1950s) women would not be expected to fight in wars and it is still not usual for them to be 'front-line' combatants. Why is this? Even here, when the girl is a soldier, she is a victim of war.
- **The pointlessness of war / Humanity**: we do not know who is fighting or why. Both sides sing the same song. It unites the girl soldier and the enemy sentinel.
- **Memory / Identity / Mental illness**: Vaudevue has lost her memory. She does not know who she is. Her mental suffering only ends with her death.
- **Death**: the attitude to death is ambiguous. Vaudevue may not be trying to kill herself, but she is seized in an 'embrace' and her suffering is over.

Form, Structure and Language

- There is a distant dream-like quality about the poem. As the poet describes the events in the **present tense** she seems to be watching from a distance.
- The water becomes **symbolic** of death. Vaudevue is drawn to the lake and its deep icy water.
- The water is **personified**. An undercurrent seizes her and dives with her. It has her in an 'embrace'. When she is dead she sleeps in the current's embrace.
- The poet uses **repetition** in lines 27–28, 37–39 and 47–48, giving the poem a hypnotic quality.
- The meaning of the repeated song title is **ambiguous**. It sounds like the kind of song people might sing in wartime urging soldiers to come home. When the sentinel plays it he could be willing Vaudevue to return from the water. It could refer to Vaudevue's 'lost' mind or perhaps death could be calling her.

next to of course god america i E. E. cummings

The Poet

E. E. cummings (1894–1962) was born in Cambridge, Massachusetts and went to Harvard University. He wrote essays and novels, but was best known for his 'modernist' poetry. He served in the American army towards the end of the First World War.

Content

Someone (probably a politician) is making a speech about men who have died in the war. He speaks of patriotism, sacrifice, glory and heroism.

Conflict

The poem was written in 1926 and does not seem to be about any particular conflict, although the poet might well be thinking of the First World War, which ended in 1918.

Ideas, Themes and Issues

- **Patriotism**: the speaker assumes that it is right to fight and die for America. He quotes the national anthem and touches on American history. He sees dying in war as something glorious because it is done for America. However, these sentiments are undermined by the nonsensical words the poet gives him.
- **Religion**: religion and patriotism are seen as being intertwined. There is assumption that God comes first and 'of course' America is next. The reference to the pilgrim fathers recalls the importance of religion in American history and politics.
- **The dead**: the speaker depicts the soldiers as being willing to die, but by calling them 'lions' gives an image of brave men whose lives have been wasted. However, there is ambiguity in the poet's attitude to the soldiers, the speaker praising them because they

didn't stop to 'think'. There could be an implication that if they had thought, they would not have fought.

Form, Structure and Language

- The **inverted commas** show us that the speaker is not the poet. The final line confirms this.
- The 'speech' is written in **lower case**. Cummings often did this. Here it has the effect of making us question the importance of God and America, in spite of the speaker's words.
- The poem is a **satire** on patriotism, criticising it by making it seem ridiculous.
- This effect is achieved partly by the use of childish words and phrases, in line 8, and **nonsensical words** like 'gorry'. This gives the sense that everything the speaker says is nonsense.
- The **forced rhymes** also undermine the sentiments, making them seem ridiculous.
- The 'speech' contains **no punctuation** until the final **question mark**, which, taken with the final line, gives the sense of someone who does not stop to draw breath – or perhaps even to think.
- The speaker uses a quotation from the national anthem and other **rhetorical clichés** in lines 7 and 13. These phrases seem glib and insincere.
- He takes a common **image**, 'lambs to the slaughter' and replaces the word 'lambs' with 'lions', unwittingly creating a powerful image which makes the soldiers' deaths seem even more tragic.
- The form of the poem is **a variation on the sonnet form**, with two **quatrains**, with alternative lines rhyming, followed by a **sestet** with a more unusual **rhyme scheme**.

Hawk Roosting Ted Hughes

The Poet

See page 64.

Content

A bird of prey 'roosts' (settles down for sleep) high in a wood. It reflects on its position high above the earth and the wonder of its own creation. It has the power to kill whenever it pleases. This has never changed and the hawk intends to keep things as they are.

Conflict

The hawk is a killer, but there is no real sense of conflict here. It simply attacks and kills, without resistance. The hawk could be seen as a symbol of both the power of nature and of powerful humans who use violence to achieve their aims and cannot be resisted. The poet himself has described the hawk as being like a Nazi.

Ideas, Themes and Issues

- **The power of nature**: the hawk is a bird of prey. It has power over other creatures and lives to kill. Nature is violent and untamed.
- **Creation**: there is a semi-religious tone to the poem. The word 'Creation' is given a capital letter. The hawk wonders at how he was made and is seen as being at the same time a product of, and the ruler of, Creation.

- **Human power**: some critics see this poem as a metaphor for political or military power and the hawk as representing dictators. The hawk is arrogant and sees himself as all-powerful. He can kill as he wishes and will not allow change. He could be seen as deluding himself. He cannot really hold creation in his foot.
- **Reason and instinct**: the hawk does not argue or discuss. He kills through instinct. He seems to despise human rationality as a weakness.
- **Death**: the hawk has the power of life and death over others, but does not acknowledge his own mortality. It has been suggested that he represents death itself.

Form, Structure and Language

- The poem is written in the **first person**. The poet adopts the **persona** of the hawk.
- His language is that of an educated, reasonable human, which **contrasts** with the sentiments he is expressing. Expressions like those in lines 5 and 7 using the terms 'convenience' and 'advantage' make him sound like an expert, carefully explaining how he does his job. He speaks of 'sophistry', which is clever, but false reasoning, and argument, but says he is not concerned with these. Far from being a rational thinker, he is a creature of instinct.
- This **contrasts** with the diction of violence and death used to describe his actions in lines 16 and 19.
- There are six **stanzas** of four lines each. This **regularity** reflects the calmness and rationality of the hawk, containing and controlling the violence.
- The hawk can be seen as a **symbol** of many things: human power; the power of nature; divine power; even death.
- The poet's attitude to his subject is not stated. The hawk is allowed a voice and is not contradicted. Readers may be impressed by his certainty or repelled by it, or both.

Preparation Task

Hawk Roosting has been interpreted in many different ways. Look on the Internet or in a library for reviews and critical essays. Compare them and think about which of them you agree with.

Try doing the same thing with other poems in the anthology.

Cluster 4: Relationships

The fifteen poems in Cluster 4 are about relationships. The earliest was written in the 17th Century and the latest in the 21st Century. Some are written by men and some by women.

The poems cover many different kinds of relationships between human beings and each poet has his or her own way of looking at the subject. In the exam you will have to make connections between poems, looking at differences and similarities in the subject matter, and in the ways in which the poets present their ideas.

The relationships, some real and some imagined, that inspired these poems are as varied as the poems themselves. Many of them are about romantic or sexual love between two people. However, they focus on different kinds of love and different stages in the relationships.

In *To His Coy Mistress*, the poet is trying to seduce a woman. The writers of *Hour* and *Ghazal* write about what it means to be in love and have that love returned. In *Sonnet 116*, Shakespeare considers the meaning of true love and what makes a love that lasts. *The Manhunt* is also about lasting love, this time tested by circumstances.

There are also relationships that have gone wrong, for example, in *The Farmer's Bride* and *Quickdraw*. *Sister Maude* is addressed to the person who has destroyed the speaker's romance and is as much about sisters as lovers. *Nettles* and *Praise Song for my Mother* are also about family, but these are much warmer relationships. In *Born Yesterday* the poet addresses a baby whom he has not even seen, yet it is one of the most touching poems in the anthology.

A great range of moods and emotions is covered in the poems, from overwhelming love to disappointment to anger. Some are serious or tragic. Others are comic.

The poets also employ a range of techniques. Many are written in the first person. In some of the poems the poets speak as themselves, while in others they adopt personae, inventing a character and imagining his or her feelings. Some use traditional poetic forms, such as the sonnet, while others write in free verse. Some poets use a lot of imagery and extravagant language, while others prefer to express their feelings in a plainer style.

These poets explore a wide variety of ideas, themes and issues. Here are just some of the common themes touched on in this cluster:

- **Romantic love**: *Hour*, *Ghazal*, *Sonnet 116*, *Sonnet 43*, *To His Coy Mistress*.
- **Sexual / Physical love**: *The Manhunt*, *In Paris with You*, *To His Coy Mistress*, *The Farmer's Bride*.
- **Family**: *Harmonium*, *Sister Maude*, *Nettles*, *Praise Song for My Mother*, *Brothers*.
- **Children**: *Praise Song for My Mother*, *Nettles*, *Born Yesterday*, *Brothers*.
- **Men and women**: *To His Coy Mistress*, *The Farmer's Bride*, *Sister Maude*.
- **Nature**: *Ghazal*, *Praise Song for My Mother*, *The Farmer's Bride*, *Nettles*.
- **Time**: *Hour*, *Harmonium*, *Sonnet 116*, *To His Coy Mistress*, *Born Yesterday*.
- **Death**: *Praise Song for My Mother*, *Sonnet 116*, *To His Coy Mistress*, *Sister Maude*, *Sonnet 43*, *Harmonium*.

Helpful Hint

You do not have to pretend you like all these poems – no one is going to like all of them. You are expected to comment on a poet's themes and techniques, but you should also give a personal response. If that poem does not work for you, it is fine to say so – just as long as you can justify your opinion using evidence from the text.

The Manhunt Simon Armitage

The Poet

Simon Armitage was born in Huddersfield, Yorkshire. After studying in Portsmouth and Manchester he worked as a probation officer and a DJ before becoming a writer. He still lives in Yorkshire. Many of his poems contain references to aspects of life in the North of England, as well as to his own family background. He has recently written poetry for television documentaries.

Content

The wife of a wounded soldier speaks of how she has gradually got to know her husband again. She touches his body, tracing the places where he has been wounded. At last she looks into the cause of his mental scarring.

Relationships

This poem is based on someone's real experience. It was originally written for a Channel 4 documentary *Forgotten Heroes: The Not Dead*, which focused on three soldiers from different wars, all of whom suffer from post traumatic stress disorder. Armitage based his poems on their experiences. This poem uses the experience of Laura, the wife of a man called Eddie, who had been wounded on peace-keeping duties in Bosnia in the 1990s. His experiences have changed him, making him difficult to live with, but she tries to understand and help him.

Ideas, Themes and Issues

- **War**: this poem could fit just as well into the 'Conflict' section. It is about the results of war and its effect on individuals – those who take part and their loved ones.
- **Change**: the man's experiences have changed him forever. As a result of this, his relationship with his wife has changed. A long-term, committed relationship means adapting to change.
- **Physical love**: Laura starts to get to know her husband again through exploring his body. Then she tries to delve into his mind. Their love is expressed physically as well as mentally.
- **The human mind**: the man's mental scars are more painful than his physical scars. Eddie has been changed forever by things he witnessed in Bosnia and could do nothing about. How can the human mind cope with such horrors?
- **Loyalty**: Laura cannot fully understand what is going on in her husband's mind, but she stands by him, showing her commitment to their marriage.

Form, Structure and Language

- Armitage adopts a **female persona**. He conveys her feelings and her confusion.
- It is a long poem and is not divided into stanzas. Laura's experience is **continuous**, one thing leading to another. The uneven length of the lines might reflect her hesitancy and caution.
- He uses a series of **metaphors** to describe the man's wounded body. Many of these have **military connotations**, for example, on lines 12 and 23.
- **Comparing** him to inanimate objects makes her exploration of him seem impersonal: he is like an object without feelings.
- Then she feels his 'grazed' heart. She uses the body part as a symbol. The two very short lines mark a change in her experience. She is now beginning to recapture feelings, trying to understand things she cannot literally feel.

Hour Carol Ann Duffy

The Poet

Carol Ann Duffy was born in Glasgow in 1955 and moved to Stafford at the age of six. She studied at Liverpool University, where she took part in poetry readings. She is often seen as a feminist poet, writing about women's experiences, and in 2009 became Britain's first female Poet Laureate.

Content

The poet speaks about an hour she spent with her lover.

Relationships

The poem is taken from a collection of love poems, *Rapture*, which traces a love affair from first meeting to breaking up. This poem tries to capture a moment of happiness, of being in love. There are no details about the identity of the people involved. According to the poet, it is written from her own experience but it could be about anyone's experience of being in love.

Ideas, Themes and Issues

- **Being in love**: this poem celebrates the joy of love. At this point in the relationship, both partners are happy. There are no complications or threats to the relationship, except for time.
- **Time**: the poem is about a single hour. Although it is a short time, love can make it seem to last forever. Time slows when you are in love. The poet sees time as the enemy of love but love can transform lives, like spinning gold out of straw.
- **True love**: the poet rejects the clichés of romance. Her love is down-to-earth and natural. It is not materialistic but provides its own (metaphorical) riches.

Form, Structure and Language

- The poem is in the form of a **sonnet**, the form used by Shakespeare and other poets for their love poetry, but in some ways Duffy departs from the usual form.
- It has fourteen lines. Like a Shakespearean sonnet it consists of three **quatrains** and a **rhyming couplet**. Unlike Shakespeare and most other poets, Duffy has divided her sonnet into **stanzas**, making the reader pause between sections.
- Most of the poem follows the **rhyme scheme** of the Shakespearean sonnet. However, Duffy uses half **rhyme**, softening the line ends in the second and fourth lines of each of the first three stanzas.

- The **rhythm** is less regular than, and not as strong as, the **iambic pentameter** of the Shakespearean sonnet. This makes the poem seem more casual and **conversational in tone**.
- The poem is in the **present tense**, reflecting the sentiments of the poem – that the present is what matters.
- Duffy uses the **first person plural** 'we' to include the object of the poem.
- She uses the **clichéd images** of romance – flowers, wine, candles – and **contrasts** them with the everyday realities of a ditch, grass and cuckoo spit.
- She uses **images** taken from legend and fairytale in lines 6 and 14 to express the strength and timelessness of the emotion.
- The value and preciousness of love is reflected in the use of words like 'treasure' and 'gold'.
- Time is **personified**, as the enemy of love, as it is in poems such as *To His Coy Mistress* (see page 80).

In Paris with You James Fenton

The Poet

James Fenton grew up in Lincolnshire and Staffordshire. He worked as a foreign correspondent and a political journalist and has used this experience in his poetry. Many of his poems are about the relationship between cultures, but he also writes love poetry and comic verse.

Content

In Paris the speaker tells his companion that he does not want to talk about love. He admits that he is angry about the past. He says he does not care where this relationship is going. He does not want to go out and see the sights, preferring to stay in the hotel room.

Relationships

As the speaker is on the rebound it would seem that this relationship has not been going on for long. He does not want to describe it as 'love' or to think about the past or the future. We do not know who the couple are or why they are in Paris. With the 'sleazy' room and the apparent lack of emotion, it sounds like a fairly casual relationship, perhaps what used to be called 'a dirty weekend'.

Ideas, Themes and Issues

- **Love and sex**: the speaker sees love as something negative because of the hurt it has caused him in the past. He does not want to describe his current relationship as 'love'. Does he want a sexual relationship with no emotion?
- **Past and future**: he has been hurt in the past, seeing himself as 'wounded'. His experience has made him wary of relationships.
- **Place**: Paris is not just any place. It brings with it connotations of love and romance.

Form, Structure and Language

- The poem is written in the **first person**, with the speaker addressing someone we take to be his lover.
- The language is **colloquial**, giving the impression that we are hearing one side of a conversation.
- There are six **stanzas**, the start of each one, apart from stanzas three and four, signalling a change of **mood** or idea. Time could be passing between stanzas.
- The third and fourth stanzas are much shorter than the others and flow into each other (using **enjambment**) Here the speaker's focus changes from his negative feelings to Paris itself and he seems to calm down.
- The poet uses rhyme, including **internal rhyme** for **comic effect**. He even makes up a word to rhyme with 'wounded'. These **longer rhymes**, in which both syllables of a word rhyme and the stress is on the first syllable, are known as '**feminine rhymes**'
- The **tone** of this poem is constantly changing. It is angry, sad, comic, romantic and ironic.
- He plays on the idea of Paris being a city of romance. He is literally in Paris with his lover but in the final stanza he uses the word 'Paris' as a substitute for 'love'. Is he falling in love and does not want to say the word because of his past? Or does 'Paris' mean something other than love?

Quickdraw Carol Ann Duffy

The Poet

See page 71.

Content

The speaker has two telephones, one a mobile and the other a landline. Her lover rings and 'wounds' her. The next time, she tries to speak first but 'misses' and the other person hits her again. She says that it is like being in a Western, with the phones standing in for guns. The lover texts and she finds the phone. She has been sent kisses.

Relationships

Like *Hour*, this poem is taken from Duffy's collection of love poems, *Rapture*, which traces the progress of a love affair. In this poem the speaker and her lover are having a fight. The speaker is hurt by the other person's words, but by the end they seem to make up.

Ideas, Themes and Issues

- **Love as a battle**: love is not always easy. Here, the couple falls out. Perhaps cracks are appearing in the relationship or perhaps it is just a lovers' tiff. They make up at the end but the kisses are 'bullets'. They too can wound.
- **Modern relationships**: today relationships are made and broken using technology. Does easy communication make things better or worse?
- Essentially, this is a very simple poem, not much more than a **joke**. Perhaps the poet is showing that there is a lighter side to love.

Form, Structure and Language

- The poet speaks directly to her lover, using the **present tense** throughout to make the poem seem more immediate.
- Each of the four **stanzas** contains four lines, though the second and third stanzas start with short lines preceded by spaces. This gives a sense of the speaker catching her breath and recovering.
- The mixture of **enjambment and pauses** in the middle of lines adds to this 'stop start' effect.
- She plays with one dominant **image**, seeing the argument as a shoot out in the Wild West.
- The poem starts with a **simile**: she wears the phones like guns.
- As the poem goes on she turns this into an **extended metaphor**: a voice is a pellet; a tongue is

a trigger, etc. This sort of fanciful **comparison** is sometimes called a **conceit**.
- Duffy refers to Western or cowboy films, such as *High Noon*.
- She uses **internal rhymes**, helping to give a light-hearted **tone** to the poem.
- She brings the poem and the argument to an end using **repetition** and **ellipsis**, suggesting that the kisses go on and on.

Helpful Hint

The first time you refer to a poet in an essay, use his or her full name, e.g. Carol Ann Duffy. From then onwards, use just the surname, e.g. Duffy, or call him / her 'the poet'. Never use the first name alone. 'Carol Ann' is not your friend!

Ghazal Mimi Khalvati

The Poet

Mimi Khalvati was born in Tehran, Iran (formerly Persia), but grew up on the Isle of Wight. She has worked as an actor and theatre director both in Britain and Iran. She started writing poetry while bringing up her children. Although she writes in English, she is influenced by both the Persian and English poetic traditions.

Content

The poet speaks to someone she loves in a series of images. She urges him to love her, showing qualities and characteristics that complement hers. If their love affair ends, she wants the relationship to continue in another way, with him as her friend, her muse, her lover or her guide.

A ghazal is a traditional Persian love poem. In the final couplet, Khalvati pays tribute to the 13th-century Persian poet, Rumi, who also wrote ghazals.

Relationships

It is not clear whether the poet's love is returned. She could be writing about a relationship that she is already involved in or about one she wants to have. Whichever it is, her feelings are very intense and physical. However, at the end she acknowledges that the relationship might change in the future.

Ideas, Themes and Issues

- **Nature**: most of the images are taken from nature. The lovers seem to be at one with nature.
- **Love**: her love is intense and all-consuming. She demands that her lover returns her love, which is physical as well as spiritual.
- **Poetry / Culture**: by writing in this form the poet pays tribute to Persian tradition and culture. She also acknowledges the power of poetry.

Form, Structure and Language

- Khalvati closely follows the traditional form of the **ghazal**. Forms like this and the sonnet, perhaps the European equivalent, present a challenge to the poet. She has to express her feelings within strict boundaries.
- A ghazal consists of at least **five couplets**. Here, there are ten. Each line has to be the same length.
- The first **couplet rhymes** (here Khalvati ends both lines with the same word), its second line introducing a **refrain**. Here, just the final word ('me') is repeated at the end of each stanza.
- She also **rhymes** the penultimate word of each couplet. This sort of rhyme is called a **mosaic rhyme**.
- A ghazal traditionally includes the poet's 'signature' in the final couplet. As a homage to Rumi, the poet refers to this tradition, including his name and that of his lover instead of her own name, in the penultimate couplet.
- Khalvati takes her **imagery** from nature, imagining both herself and her lover taking on different forms to express their relationship.

Brothers Andrew Forster

The Poet

Andrew Forster grew up in South Yorkshire but now lives in Scotland, where he works as a Literature Development Officer. His first collection of poetry was published in 2007. He draws on his own experience, with poems based on his childhood, but also writes about real and imagined figures from the past.

Content

The poet remembers going out with his two brothers one afternoon. The youngest boy, aged six, had to go home to get his bus fare from their mother. As the bus arrived the two older boys ran for it, leaving their brother behind.

Relationships

There are three brothers in the poem. The poet, at nine, is a year younger than Paul, the oldest. They seem to have a close relationship. The other boy, however, is quite a lot younger and they resent being made to look after him.

The poet sees the incident as representing a time when he started to grow apart from his younger brother.

Ideas, Themes and Issues

- **Families**: the poem presents a picture of an ordinary family. The brothers' relationship is fairly typical of boys of that age. 'Mum' is a presence in the background and the family would seem to be secure and unexceptional.
- **Childhood**: the poet looks back from the viewpoint of an adult. He remembers vividly exactly what it was like to be nine years old, but he now understands the relationships and what his actions meant.
- **Growing up**: the speaker and his brother Paul are very conscious that they are older. They feel grown up, being able to go to town on the bus, doing things grown-ups do.
- **The past / Memories**: the poet tries to recapture a significant moment in the past. Does he regret putting distance between himself and his younger brother?

Form, Structure and Language

- The poet addresses his younger brother directly, using the **second person**. He uses the past tense as he recalls events from a long time ago
- The poem is divided into three **stanzas**. The first describes the situation, the three brothers apparently in harmony. In the second stanza, things change

when the six-year-old boy has to go back home and the two older brothers silently agree to leave him. In the final stanza the bus comes and the distance opens up between the boys.
- The third stanza is shorter than the other two. The poet does not explain or discuss his present relationship with his brother, but leaves us to draw our own conclusions.
- He uses **non-Standard English**, reflecting everyday speech, for example, in line 1.
- He refers to details that place the experience in a real time and place. The boys talk about local football teams; the young boy wears a tank top.
- The word 'distance' in the final stanza is both **literal** and **metaphorical**. Running for the bus, the poet increases the distance between himself and his younger brother. In retrospect, the action seems to be an **epiphany**, symbolising the emotional distance that would grow between them.

Practice Question

Answer this Foundation Tier question in 45 minutes. Answer both parts (a) and (b).

Part (a) What does the speaker feel about family relationships in 'Brothers'?
Part (b) Compare the ways that families are shown in this poem and one other poem from 'Relationships'.

Praise Song for My Mother Grace Nichols

The Poet

Grace Nichols was born in Guyana in the West Indies in 1950. She worked as a teacher and journalist before settling in Britain in 1977. As well as poems she writes children's stories, which are often based on Guyanese folklore and legends.

Content

The poet looks back on what her mother meant to her. She thinks about what her mother wanted for her.

Relationships

The relationship between mother and daughter is expressed from the daughter's point of view. We can assume her mother is dead from the use of the past tense. Her feelings are entirely positive, appropriately for a 'praise song', a kind of eulogy. No details are given about the woman's, or her daughter's, life.

Ideas, Themes and Issues

- **Motherhood**: the poem expresses the deep bond between a mother and her child. The mother was the child's whole world, giving her life and nourishing her.
- **Nature**: this bond is expressed through images of nature. The mother is in harmony with nature.
- **Heritage and culture**: the mother represents the poet's past. She is associated with animals and plants that are native to the place where she lived and where her daughter was born.
- **Growing up and moving on**: the poet's mother is dead but her daughter can move forward because she was encouraged by her mother to go to her 'futures'. The relationship has given her the ability to do this.

Form, Structure and Language

- Praise songs are traditional African poems or songs consisting of a series of **epithets** (**descriptions**) in praise of something or someone, such as a king or military leader. Professional praise singers perform these songs in public.
- The poem is addressed directly to the mother, using the **second person** ('you') – traditional in a praise song.
- The first three stanzas follow a **regular pattern**, each having three lines and the same grammatical structure: the first line is 'you were'; the second says what she was, using a **noun**, and adding 'to me'; and the third expands on it with a **noun phrase**. The fourth stanza is longer, adding one **comparison** to another and building up the emotion. The final, one-line stanza, is **simple and direct**.
- **Repetition** makes it sound like a **ritualistic chant** or **song**.
- The poet uses a series of **metaphors** to express her feelings about her mother. These are all taken from nature. The first three – the sea, the moon and the sunrise – are universal: any reader could identify with them and their meaning. The four **images** in the fourth stanza are more particular and recall the poet's childhood in the West Indies.

Practice Question

Answer this Higher Tier question within 45 minutes.

Q How do poets use imagery to present ideas about relationships in *Praise Song for My Mother* and one other poem from 'Relationships'?

Harmonium Simon Armitage

The Poet

See page 70.

Content

The poet remembers being offered a harmonium (a sort of small organ), which was being thrown out by a local church. It had been used in worship for a hundred years in the church where both he and his father had sung in the choir. Now his father comes to help him carry it out of the church and remarks that the next box his son will carry out of the church will be his coffin.

Relationships

The harmonium represents the bond between father and son, and the life and heritage they have in common. The incident also shows the kind of relationship they have, which might be thought fairly typical between adult men and their fathers. Although they are quite close and do things together, they do not express their feelings directly: 'he, being him… And I, being me…'.

Ideas, Themes and Issues

- **The past**: the harmonium is being thrown out, a relic of the past. It evokes memories of the poet's childhood.
- **Heritage and culture**: music and religion are intertwined in the poet's background. His family's association with the church goes back generations. He grew up in a society where both church-going and singing in choirs were important parts of community life. Is the fact that the harmonium is no longer wanted a symptom of the disappearance of a way of life?
- **Old age and death**: the poet's father jokes about his son coming back to the church to carry his coffin. Reminders of the past sharpen his awareness of what will happen in the future.

Form, Structure and Language

- The poem centres on an **anecdote** about an ordinary, undramatic event, which makes the poet think about his past and his relationship with his father.
- It is arranged in four **stanzas** of varying lengths. The first simply states the situation; the second describes the state of the instrument; the third says what it means to him; and the final stanza (in the **present tense**) focuses on his father.
- The poet uses some **specialised diction** to describe the harmonium, as well as **musical terms**. He plays with the **double meanings** of phrases such as 'for a song' and 'struck a chord'. References to 'harmonics' and the word 'harmonium' itself might make us think about harmony between father and son.
- The harmonium becomes a **symbol** of the relationship, of the past and of the community.
- The **sound** of the words is important, reflecting the sound of the organ and choir. There is **alliteration**: 'hummed harmonics' and **assonance**: 'opened their throats'.
- There is a mood of **nostalgia**. Memories are described using rich, almost fantastic **imagery**: the sun raising the dead and finches flying from the choristers' mouths.
- The poem ends with a **rhyming couplet**, which does not give a neat ending, as might be expected, but leaves us with the sense that the experience – and the relationship – is over too soon, before the poet can say what he wants to say.

Sonnet 43 Elizabeth Barrett Browning

The Poet

Elizabeth Barrett (1806–1861) came from a wealthy family. She had respiratory problems and suffered a spinal injury from a riding accident. After the death of her mother and brother she became increasingly housebound. She began to publish poetry, however, and her work came to the attention of poet Robert Browning. After exchanging letters for some time, they met and, against her father's wishes, married. They went to Italy, where she continued to write poetry whilst campaigning against child labour and slavery, and for women's rights.

Content

The poet recounts to her lover the ways in which she loves him. This poem is one of 50 from the poet's *Sonnets from the Portuguese*, which were written between meeting and marrying Robert Browning.

Relationships

This poem, although addressed to a person, does not directly tell us very much about either the speaker or the person being addressed, although the deaths of the poet's mother and brother are referred to. It tries to describe what her feelings are like.

The love is deep and seems to dominate the speaker's life, but it could be the love of any one person for any other. Perhaps this is why it is so popular and is often used at weddings.

Ideas, Themes and Issues

- **The nature of love**: Barrett Browning does not write about the man she loves, but about love itself. She tries to explain what this love is like by comparing it to other experiences and feelings, from the quietness of everyday life, through political and moral principles to grief and religious faith.
- **Spirituality and religion**: the poet sees her love as something spiritual, going hand in hand with her religious beliefs. At the end of the poem she places her love and the future in God's hands.
- **Death**: she refers to the deaths of her loved ones and how she felt she would not love again. Love overcomes grief and might even outlast her own death and that of her lover.

Form, Structure and Language

- The poet speaks directly to her lover, using the **first and second persons**. The use of the **archaic** 'thee' helps to give the poem a reverent, **religious** feel.
- The poem is in the form of a **sonnet**, consisting of 14 lines. It is closer in form to the **Petrarchan**, or Italian **sonnet**, than the Shakespearean sonnet.
- It is divided into two parts, The first, of eight lines, is known as an **octave** and the second, of six lines, as a **sestet**. There is no real division between the contents of the two parts, but in the sestet the emotions become stronger.
- Like Shakespeare's sonnets, it is written in **iambic pentameter**, the regular rhythm of the human heart.
- The poet uses **hyperbole** (exaggeration) to try to express how great her love is by comparing it to other emotions and feelings.
- The **religious diction** makes the poem almost prayer-like and the love holy: 'soul'; 'Grace'; 'saints'. Both language and content reflect the poet's Christian faith.

Sonnet 116 William Shakespeare

The Poet

William Shakespeare (1564–1616) is widely thought of as the greatest writer who ever lived.

He was born and died in Stratford-upon-Avon, but spent most of his life in London.

He wrote over 30 plays, several long poems and more than a hundred sonnets, adapting the popular Italian form of love poetry to create what is now known as the Shakespearean sonnet.

Content

The poet writes about the nature of true and lasting love. He says that it survives problems, difficulties and the passing of time.

Relationships

Shakespeare's sonnets are usually addressed to a specific person, the object of his love.

This sonnet discusses love itself, although the poet may be thinking of a particular relationship. He is clearly talking about a long-term relationship – 'the marriage of true minds'.

Whether it is an actual marriage is not clear, but it is a love which is constant and unchanging.

Ideas, Themes and Issues

- **True love**: the poet sees romantic love as something deep and lasting. It is not based on youth and beauty, but outlasts them. It can overcome 'impediments' and does not change whatever problems arise.
- **Time and change**: the poet is aware of mortality and the passing of time, but sees love as lasting even beyond death, 'even to the edge of doom'.

Form, Structure and Language

- All Shakespeare's **sonnets** follow the same form. It is almost a set of rules which he sets himself. Elizabethans liked to demonstrate their ability to use such forms effectively, almost like a game. The **strict pattern** also helps to organise the poet's thoughts and feelings.
- There are fourteen lines, arranged into three **quatrains** (sets of four lines of **alternate rhymes**), followed by a **rhyming couplet**. In the first quatrain, Shakespeare states his case about love, saying that

love which changes easily is not love. In the second he says that, on the contrary, love is fixed and unchanging. In the third he makes a statement about love and time, asserting that true love is eternal. He ends with a resounding **rhyming couplet** that challenges anyone to contradict him.

- Like all Shakespeare's sonnets, the poem is written in **iambic pentameter**, a meter said to imitate the beat of the human heart.
- To capture the essence of true love, he uses **metaphors** that compare love to a fixed 'mark' or target, buffeted by storms, and to the polestar, which sailors rely on to guide them to their destination.
- Love and time are both **personified**. Love is able to resist time, which may take away youth and beauty but cannot harm love itself. The **image** of time with a sickle is a common one.
- The **tone** of the poem is confident and sincere as the poet asserts his beliefs and perhaps his own love.
- Although most of the sonnet is rather **impersonal**, with neither 'you' nor 'I' used in the first twelve lines, the last two lines suggest that this is a deeply held view based on personal experience.

To His Coy Mistress Andrew Marvell

The Poet

Andrew Marvell (1621–1678) was born near Hull in Yorkshire. After going to Cambridge University, he got involved in politics. This was the time of the English Civil War and Marvell was a keen republican, opposed to the King. In 1659 he was elected as MP for Hull.

Content

A 'mistress' in Marvell's time meant the woman whom a man loved, sometimes one who did not return his love. Here the poet uses humour, fear and logical argument to try to seduce his mistress, telling her that they have to make the most of the time they have.

Relationships

The poet seems to love the woman. He certainly wants to seduce her. We do not know whether she returns his love but he seems to think she does and that she is playing with his affections, resisting him through 'coyness' – pretending to be shy. He wants a physical, not just a romantic, relationship.

Ideas, Themes and Issues

- **Love and sex**: the poet is not satisfied with unrequited love. He says that he would wait for her forever if it were possible, but it is not. He urges her to give up her virginity and enjoy life.
- **Time and mortality**: he wants to make the most of life because he is aware that it is so short. He knows he cannot defy time and death, but knowing how short life is makes it all the more important to enjoy it while he can.

Form, Structure and Language

- The poet speaks directly to his mistress, using the **first and second person**.
- There are three **stanzas** of different lengths. In the first he explains what he and his mistress would do 'had we but world enough, and time'. In the second stanza, he argues that they do not have time. In the third he tells her what he thinks they should do. The poem is constructed as a **logical argument**.
- The lines are quite short. The use of **iambic tetrameter** (four beats to a line with the stress on every second syllable), combined with the **rhyming couplets**, give the poem a **light-hearted tone** despite the serious subject matter.
- The first stanza is **satirical** in **tone**. The idea of eternal unfulfilled love is made quite **comical** by the use of **contrast** (the Humber and the Ganges), unusual **imagery** ('vegetable love') and **hyperbole** ('A hundred years should go to praise…')
- Time is **personified** in a powerful and very famous image; 'Time's winged chariot hurrying near'.
- The **imagery** of the second stanza is powerful and macabre, using **vocabulary** associated with death ('marble vault'; 'worms'; 'ashes') to create a horrifying picture.
- In **contrast**, the final stanza uses **imagery** that suggests youthful health and strength, such as the **simile** 'like amorous birds of prey'. It is not exaggerated and 'poetic' like the **imagery** of the first stanza, but seems real, down-to-earth and vigorous. He wants them to 'tear out pleasures with rough strife'.

The Farmer's Bride Charlotte Mew

The Poet

Charlotte Mew (1869–1928) was born in London, the daughter of a successful architect. Her poetry and short stories were much admired at the time, particularly by fellow writers such as Thomas Hardy. However, she was haunted by the fear of mental illness, two of her siblings having been committed to institutions. She killed herself by drinking poison.

Content

A farmer tells the story of his marriage to a young woman. He says that as soon as they were married she became afraid of him and everything human. He says she was more like a fay (or fairy) than a human being. One night she ran away, so the farmer and his friends chased her across the fields to the town and brought her back home. Since then, she does the housework and plays with animals but will not let men near her. With Christmas coming he thinks about how there will be no children in the house. His bride sleeps alone in the attic.

Relationships

In a sense, there is no relationship in this poem. Although they are married, the farmer and his bride cannot communicate. She is afraid of him and other men, perhaps afraid of sex. He finds her so difficult to understand that he thinks she must be a fairy. He longs for her physically but cannot have her.

Ideas, Themes and Issues

- **Marriage**: this is a strange marriage. The farmer 'chose a maid'. Perhaps it is a 'marriage of convenience', the farmer needing a wife to help him.
- **Sexual desire**: the bride is completely innocent. As soon as she is married she becomes afraid of the farmer, which he cannot understand. The poem ends with his anguish at wanting her sexually but not being able to have her.
- **Men and women**: the sexes seem poles apart in this poem. The men chase the woman and lock her up. She remains a mystery to them. Are women only there for sex and housework? Could this poem be about all men and all women, not just a farmer and a 'fay'?
- **Nature**: the bride is compared to animals, birds and trees. The farmer is aware of nature and the passing of the seasons.

Form, Structure and Language

- Mew adopts a **male persona**, giving a voice to the farmer, but keeping the bride a mystery.
- The first two **stanzas** are in the **past tense** and tell the story of the farmer and his bride. The next four, in the **present tense**, tell us about how they live now.
- There is **strong regular rhythm**, each line containing four stressed syllables until the very last line, which is lengthened by the **repeated** 'her hair' as the farmer struggles to control his feelings.
- Mew uses **rhyming couplets**, which may reflect the apparent simplicity of the farmer. However, she varies the **rhyme scheme** slightly from stanza to stanza. Why?
- The farmer speaks in the **dialect** of a countryman from the West of England: 'she runned away'; 'her be'; 'more's to do'.
- The poet uses a series of **similes** comparing the bride to nature: 'shy as a leveret'; 'sweet as the wild violets'. This reflects both his character and situation – he compares her to things he knows – and his perception of her as a wild inhuman thing, belonging to nature.

Sister Maude Christina Rossetti

The Poet

Christina Rossetti (1830–1894) was one of the most popular poets of the Victorian age. She was born in London to an Italian family.

Her brother, the painter Dante Gabriel Rossetti, was a leading figure in the Pre-Raphaelite movement. Like the Pre-Raphaelites, Christina Rossetti was drawn to gothic and medieval themes.

Content

A woman blames her sister for telling their parents about her secret love affair. The lover is now dead (presumably killed on the orders of the woman's father). She blames her sister's actions on jealousy.

She says that her parents might go to Heaven when they die. Even she and her lover might be allowed in, but Maude is too wicked to be saved.

Relationships

There are a number of relationships in this poem. The speaker has had a love affair, which her parents did not approve of. It seems likely that they did not approve of the man, although it could just be that they did not approve of the affair itself: she refers to 'my shame'. Although the parents seem to have ordered the man's death, she is willing to forgive them. Her anger is reserved for her sister, Maude.

Ideas, Themes and Issues

- **Family life**: the woman has been hurt by those closest to her. Her parents may have acted in what they thought were her best interests or they may have been putting their own reputation first. Whatever the reason, love has turned to hate.
- **Betrayal**: the speaker has been betrayed by her own sister. She thinks that Maude acted out of jealousy.
- **Men and women / Sexual morality**: the woman speaks of 'shame'. Rossetti might be alluding to the 'double standards' of Victorian morality, when women who had sex outside marriage would be thought of as 'fallen' and bear the burden of guilt and shame.
- **Love**: her love is forbidden but it is strong. It lives on after her lover's death.
- **Forgiveness**: the speaker seems to embrace the Christian idea of forgiveness – God will forgive her, her lover and her parents. However, her anger is such that she cannot forgive her sister.

Form, Structure and Language

- The poet adopts a **persona** to address her sister directly.
- The poem is in the form of a **ballad** and, like a traditional ballad, it tells a strong **dramatic story**.
- There are five **stanzas**. The first four are **quatrains**, as in a **ballad**. The fifth has two additional lines. It is as if the poem should have ended with everyone going to Heaven, but the speaker feels compelled to add another two lines. She cannot let go of her anger.
- As in most ballads, there is a **strong regular rhyme scheme**, with every second and fourth line rhyming.
- There is a strong, mostly **regular rhythm**. Rossetti departs from the usual ballad form by varying the number of stressed syllables from time to time. In the second stanza she seems to miss a syllable, starting on the stressed 'cold'. This has a powerful dramatic effect.
- Although we do not know exactly when and where the poem is set, the **diction** suggests an historical setting, e.g. the use of the **archaic** 'comeliest' and the references to Heaven and crowns.

Nettles Vernon Scannell

The Poet

Vernon Scannell (1922–2007) was born in Lincolnshire and left school at 14. He served in the army during World War Two, was wounded and deserted twice. After the war he attended Leeds University but was arrested for desertion and put in a mental hospital. He worked as a professional boxer, a teacher and for the BBC.

Content

The poet tells the story of his young son falling into a bed of nettles. After comforting his son, he cuts down the nettles and burns them. Two weeks later new nettles have grown in their place.

Relationships

The poem is about the relationship between a father and his son, although the boy's mother seems to be present too and has a role to play: 'We soothed him…'. The father reacts to the boy's pain by first attending to him and making him feel better, and then going out to destroy the cause of the pain. However, at the end he acknowledges that, however much he might want to, a father cannot stop his son being hurt forever.

Ideas, Themes and Issues

- **Growing up**: although the child is very young at the time, this incident makes his father realise that he will grow up and 'often feel sharp wounds again'. When he is older his parents will not be able to make things better.

- **Revenge**: The father's instinctive reaction to his son's pain is to take his revenge on what caused it.
- **Man versus nature**: the nettles represent the dangerous and harmful side of nature. The poet seems to have power over nature as he destroys the nettles, but they return, showing he has no real power.
- **Family life**: the poet gives us a picture of a secure and loving family, but he also shows that there are limits to what love and care can achieve.

Form, Structure and Language

- The poem is written in the **first person** and is in the **past tense**, as the poet shares with us an incident from his family life. It could be said to be **anecdotal**.
- The single stanza consists of four **quatrains** (sets of four lines). There are four stages to the poem – the boy's accident; the boy being comforted; the father destroying the nettles; and the nettles growing back. These correspond roughly, but not exactly, to the quatrains. This, and the use of **enjambment**, help to give the poem continuity.
- There is a **regular rhyme scheme**, each quatrain rhyming *abab*.
- The poem does not have a **strong rhythm**, but it is regular, written in **iambic pentameter**. What effect does the regularity of the form have?
- The poet **personifies** the nettles and uses **military diction** to describe them, creating an **extended metaphor**. The nettles are soldiers who attack the boy but are then killed by his father. Finally, they are replaced by 'new recruits'.
- The sun and rain are **personified**, giving a sense of all of nature being against the boy and his father.
- There is a **contrast** between the **gentle language** used when the boy's pain is described ('soothed'; 'tender') and the **violent language** used when the poet attacks the nettles ('slashed in fury').

Born Yesterday Philip Larkin

The Poet

Philip Larkin (1922–1985) studied English at Oxford before becoming a librarian. He was the chief librarian at Hull University for 30 years, during which time he became one of the best known and most admired poets in Britain.

Content

The poem is subtitled *'for Sally Amis'*. The poet tells the newborn daughter of a friend, the well-known novelist Kingsley Amis, what he wants for her. He says that he is not wishing for the usual gifts that people wish for, like beauty, innocence and love. If she cannot have those things, he would like her to be 'ordinary'. Sadly, Sally Amis died at the age of 46 having suffered from alcoholism and depression for most of her adult life.

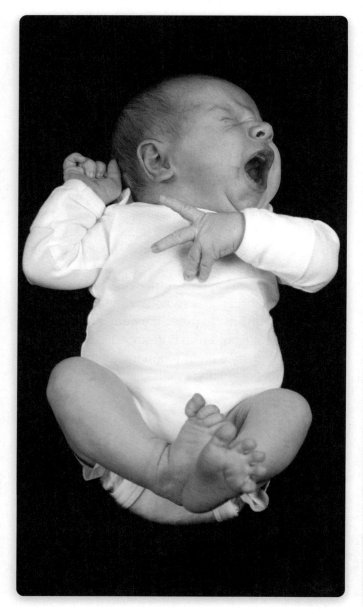

Relationships

The relationship here could be between any adult and any child, perhaps even a parent and child. But it is clear from the subtitle that the child to whom the poem is dedicated is not a close relative. His relationship is with her parents and he may not have seen the baby, but he appears to be interested in her welfare and future.

Ideas, Themes and Issues

- **Hopes and wishes**: Larkin's 'gift' to the child is reminiscent of fairytales such as *Sleeping Beauty*, where fairy godmothers visit a newborn child and bestow gifts on it. Perhaps extravagant hopes and wishes belong in fairytales, not in the real world.
- **Being ordinary**: Larkin celebrates the idea of 'ordinariness'. There is a lot to be said for being average or even 'dull'. Happiness can be achieved quietly and without drama. You might disagree with this idea.
- **Friendship**: the poem is in itself symbolic of the value of friendship.
- **Growing up / The future**: the poem gains extra poignancy from our knowledge of what happened to the real Sally. Her story makes the poet's wishes for her seem almost prophetic. Would she have been better off with a dull and uneventful life?

Form, Structure and Language

- The poem is addressed directly to the child, using the **second person**. It is a celebration of her birth, written as a gift to her and her parents.
- The **first stanza** is in the **past tense**. The poet states that he has made a wish for the child and tells her what he has not wished her. In the **second stanza** he tells her what he does want for her and explains why.
- The poem begins with a **metaphor**, which conveys both the beauty of a newborn baby and a sense of her future growth.
- The 'wishes' described in the first stanza are **clichés**: the 'usual', forming a **contrast** with the unusual wish he reveals in the second stanza.
- The poet's wishes are, at first, expressed in a **pessimistic** way. He talks about what she should not be, but in the end the poem turns apparent dullness into something good with a list of **optimistic adjectives**, making us question our perception of someone who might appear 'dull'.
- The poem ends with a **rhyming couplet**, which provides a neat conclusion as if Larkin has proved his point.

Glossary of Literary Terms

This is a list of terms that you will find useful when writing about literature.

You have probably already used most of them in class when discussing the language and techniques that writers use in their work.

It is good to be able to use these terms with confidence, but remember that you should always explain the effect a technique has on the reader (you).

Adjectives: describe nouns and add detail, e.g. 'great', 'wonderful', 'yellow'.

Adverbs: describe verbs (how the action is done). They usually end in 'ly', e.g. 'carefully', 'easily', 'quickly'.

Alliteration: repetition of a sound at the beginning of words, e.g. 'river rushing rapidly'.

Ambiguity: the effect of a word or phrase that has more than one possible meaning (i.e. it is ambiguous).

Antagonist: someone who is opposed to the protagonist.

Antithesis: the direct opposite.

Aside: a line or two addressed to the audience by a character in a play.

Assonance: repetition of a vowel sound within words, e.g. 'how now brown cow', in order to convey a mood or feeling.

Caesura: a pause in a line of poetry, usually shown by a punctuation mark.

Cliché: a phrase or opinion that is over-used.

Colloquial language: informal language; the sort of language used in conversation; may include dialect words or phrases.

Connotation: a meaning that is suggested by the use of a word or phrase because of what is associated with it, e.g. red might indicate danger.

Couplet: a pair of lines in poetry.

Dialect: words or phrases particular to a region or area.

Dialogue: conversation, especially in a play.

Diction: the kind of words and phrases used, e.g. formal diction, violent diction, technical diction.

Dramatic irony: irony of the situation, where the audience knows more than the character.

Elegy (adjective: elegiac): a poem of mourning, originally for a friend or well-known figure. It can also be a poem that reflects on death and passing time in a melancholy mood.

Elision: running a word into others, e.g. 'fish 'n' chips'.

End-stopped: brought to an end, when a line of poetry ends at the end of a sentence or clause (as opposed to enjambment).

Enjambment: when a clause or sentence runs from one line of poetry to another, i.e. not stopping at the end of the line.

Exclamations: show anger, shock, horror, surprise and joy, e.g. 'We won!'

Eye rhyme (or sight rhyme): where words look as though they rhyme but do not, e.g. 'bear' / 'fear'.

Genre: a specific type of writing, with its own conventions, e.g. detective story, romance, science fiction.

Half rhyme: an 'imperfect' rhyme – the consonants agree but the vowels do not, e.g. 'swans' / 'stones'.

Hyperbole: exaggeration.

Imagery: 'painting a picture' in words, using descriptive language, metaphors or similes.

Imperatives: commands or instructions, e.g. 'don't do that!' or 'fry for ten minutes'.

Irony and sarcasm: the use of words to imply the opposite of their meaning.

Juxtaposition: putting words or phrases (often contrasting) next to each other.

Litotes: an understatement made by denying the opposite of something (a type of irony), e.g. 'no mean feat' or 'not averse to a drink'.

Metaphor: an image created by referring to something as something else, e.g. 'an army of nettles'.

Meter: the formal arrangement of a poem's rhythm, e.g. iambic pentameter.

Naïve narrator: a story-teller who does not fully understand what is going on.

Narrator: the person telling the story.

Narrative: a story or an account of something.

Glossary of Literary Terms

Omniscient narrator: a story-teller who knows everything and, therefore, can tell us what each character is thinking and feeling.

Onomatopoeia: a word that sounds like what it describes, e.g. 'splash', 'clang', 'click'.

Oxymoron: two contradictory words placed together, e.g. 'cold fire', 'bitter sweet'.

Pathos: the emotional quality of a text or part of it, causing feelings of pity, sympathy or sadness in the reader.

Pathetic fallacy: when the surroundings (e.g. the weather) reflect the mood of a character.

Persona: a 'voice' or character adopted by a writer writing in the first person.

Personification: writing about an object, animal or idea as if it were a person, giving it human qualities, e.g. 'the wind whispered', 'time will not wait for us'.

Polemic: a written attack on an opinion or policy.

Protagonist: the main character.

Quatrain: a set of four lines of poetry.

Repetition: when words, phrases, sentences or structures are repeated.

Rhetorical question: a question which does not require an answer.

Rhythm: the beat of the writing, especially in poetry – fast or slow, regular or irregular.

Satire: writing that makes fun of people or society in order to criticise them.

Sibilance: repetition of 'hissing' sounds – 's', 'sh' and 'zh'.

Simile: a direct comparison of one thing to another, using the words 'as', 'like' or 'than', e.g. 'as big as a house', 'like an angry lion', 'faster than a speeding bullet'.

Sonnet: a poem, usually a love poem, consisting of fourteen lines.

Standard English: the conventional use of words and grammar in the English language; used in formal writing.

Structure: how a text or story is organised and arranged.

Stanza: a division in a poem; the equivalent of a paragraph in prose.

Superlatives: words that express the best of something. They usually end in 'est' or have 'most' before them, e.g. 'happiest', 'biggest', 'most beautiful'.

Symbols / symbolism: a symbol is an object that represents an idea / feeling, e.g. doves symbolise peace.

Tone: the overall feeling or attitude of the writing, e.g. formal, informal, sad, playful, angry, ironic.

Unreliable narrator: a story-teller who may not be telling us the truth.

Verse: in poetry, verse is used as an alternative to stanza.

'like an angry lion' (Simile)

List of Authors for Controlled Assessment

If you are taking the poetry exam, (Unit 2 'Poetry Across Time') you will have studied one of the clusters of poems in the anthology. In that case, you will also take Unit 3 ('The Significance of Shakespeare and the English Literary Heritage'), which is assessed by controlled assessment.

If you are not taking the poetry exam, you will take Unit 5 ('Exploring Poetry') by controlled assessment. For these two units you have a wider choice of texts, but for both you must study some work from the English Literary Heritage. The following writers' work may be studied:

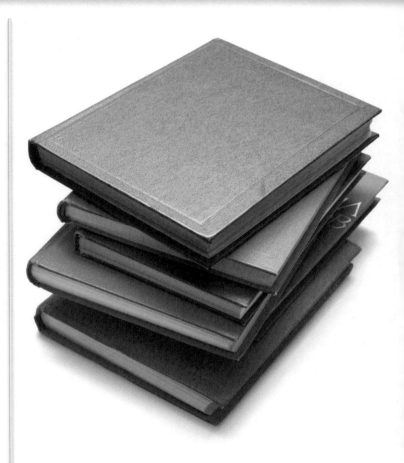

Pre-twentieth Century Poetry

Matthew Arnold
Charlotte Brontë
Robert Browning
Geoffrey Chaucer
Samuel Taylor Coleridge
John Dryden
Thomas Hardy
Robert Herrick
John Keats
Andrew Marvell
Alexander Pope
Percy Bysshe Shelley
Jonathan Swift
William Wordsworth

William Blake
Emily Brontë
Lord Byron
John Clare
John Donne
Oliver Goldsmith
George Herbert
Gerard Manley Hopkins
Christopher Marlowe
John Milton
William Shakespeare
Edmund Spenser
Henry Vaughan
Thomas Wyatt

Twentieth Century Poetry

W.H. Auden
Robert Frost
Ted Hughes
Philip Larkin
Wilfred Owen
Siegfried Sassoon
Dylan Thomas
R.S. Thomas

T.S. Eliot
Seamus Heaney
Elizabeth Jennings
D.H. Lawrence
Sylvia Plath
Stevie Smith
Edward Thomas
W.B. Yeats

Pre-twentieth Century Prose

Jane Austen
Emily Brontë
Wilkie Collins
Daniel Defoe
George Eliot
Elizabeth Gaskell
Henry James
Robert Louis Stevenson
Anthony Trollope
Oscar Wilde

Charlotte Brontë
John Bunyan
Joseph Conrad
Charles Dickens
Henry Fielding
Thomas Hardy
Mary Shelley
Jonathan Swift
H.G. Wells

Twentieth Century Prose

Kingsley Amis
William Golding
Aldous Huxley
D.H. Lawrence
George Orwell
J.B. Priestley
Stevie Smith
William Trevor
John Wyndham

E.M. Forster
Graham Greene
James Joyce
Katherine Mansfield
Sylvia Plath
Siegfried Sassoon
Muriel Spark
Evelyn Waugh

Pre-twentieth Century Drama

William Congreve
Christopher Marlowe
Richard Brinsley Sheridan

Oliver Goldsmith
William Shakespeare
Oscar Wilde

Twentieth Century Drama

T.S. Eliot
Harold Pinter
Peter Shaffer
R.C. Sherriff
Arnold Wesker

Sean O'Casey
J.B. Priestley
George Bernard Shaw
Dylan Thomas

Index

Acknowledgements

p.10–11 My Polish Teacher's Tie from Ice Cream by Helen Dunmore (Penguin 2001). Reprinted by permission of A P Watt Ltd on behalf of Helen Dunmore.

p.23 Checking Out Me History by John Agard. Reprinted by permission of the Caroline Sheldon Literary Agency.

p.26 Singh Song! by Daljit Nagra. Reprinted by permission of the publisher, Faber and Faber Ltd.

p.29 Les Grands Seigneurs by Dorothy Molloy. Reprinted by permission of the publisher, Faber and Faber Ltd.

p.36 On a Portrait of a Deaf Man by John Betjeman. © John Betjeman by permission of the Estate of John Betjeman.

p.38 The Blackbird of Glanmore by Seamus Heaney. Reprinted by permission of the publisher, Faber and Faber Ltd.

p.41 Cold Knap Lake from Collected Poems by Gillian Clarke (Carcanet, 1997). Reprinted by permission of Carcanet Press Limited.

p.42 Price We Pay for the Sun from The Fat Black Woman's Poems by Grace Nichols. Reprinted by permission of Curtis Brown Group Ltd, London on behalf of Grace Nichols.

p.44 Crossing the Loch from JIZZEN by Kathleen Jamie. Reprinted by permission of Picador, an imprint Pan Macmillan, London. Copyright © Kathleen Jamie, 1999.

p.45 Hard Water by Jean Sprackland, published by Jonathan Cape. Reprinted by permission of The Random House Group Ltd.

p.57 The Yellow Palm from King Driftwood by John Minhinnick (Carcanet, 2008). Reprinted by permission of Carcanet Press Limited.

p.58 The Right Word from The Terrorist at My Table by Imtiaz Dharker (Bloodaxe Books, 2006). Reprinted by permission of Bloodaxe Books Ltd.

p.77 Harmonium by Simon Armitage. Reprinted by permission of David Godwin Associates.

p.83 Nettles from New and Collected Poems by Vernon Scannell © Vernon Scannell. Reprinted by permission of the Literary Executor for Estate of Vernon Scannell.

p.2   ©iStockphoto.com/Pamela Cowart-Rickman

p.25   ©iStockphoto.com

p.26   ©iStockphoto.com/Chris Schmidt

p.27   ©iStockphoto.com/Eileen Hart

p.34   ©iStockphoto.com

p.41   ©iStockphoto.com/Marcus Lindström

p.42   ©iStockphoto.com/Peeter Viisimaa

p.57   ©iStockphoto.com/Timothy Pike

p.70   ©iStockphoto.com/Lukasz Kulicki

p.79   ©iStockphoto.com/Anthony Baggett

p.80   ©iStockphoto.com/Duncan Walker

All other images ©2009 Jupiterimages Corporation and Lonsdale.